Growing Vegetables in South Africa

Capel Hemy

SOUTHERN
BOOK PUBLISHERS

Copyright © 1984 by C. Hemy

All rights reserved. No part of this publication may be reproduced or transmitted in any form or by any means without prior written permission from the publisher.

ISBN 1 86812 491 6

First edition, first impression 1988
Second edition, first impression 1993
Second edition, second impression 1995
Second edition, third impression 1996

Published by
Southern Book Publishers (Pty) Ltd
PO Box 3103, Halfway House, 1685

Previously published by
Macmillan South Africa (Publishers) (Pty) Ltd

Illustrations by Shirley Greenstein

Set in Times 10.5 on 12 pt
Printed and bound by Colorgraphic, Durban

Contents

Preface 4
1. PLANNING 5
2. SITE AND CLIMATE 9
3. SOIL MANAGEMENT 15
4. WATERING 24
5. SOWING AND TRANSPLANTING 31
6. GROWING SYSTEMS 40
   Fluid sowing 40 □ Deep-beds 42 □ Spacing 44 □ Hydro-growing 46 □ Greenhouses and tunnels 46 □ Growing by the moon 47
7. SUCCESSIONAL CROPPING 50
8. CONTAINER GROWING 55
9. HARVESTING 65
10. THE BASIC VEGETABLES 75
    Basic fertilizer programme 75 □ Sowing depths 76 □ Cultivars 77 □ Yields 81 □ Basic sowing periods 82 □ Beans, broad, bush, lima, pole 83 □ Beet 89 □ Broccoli 90 □ Brussels sprouts 92 □ Cabbage 93 □ Carrot 95 □ Cauliflower 97 □ Cucumber 99 □ Eggplant 101 □ Leek 103 □ Lettuce 104 □ Melon 107 □ New Zealand spinach 109 □ Onion 110 □ Parsley 113 □ Parsnip 114 □ Pea 116 □ Pepper 117 □ Potato 119 □ Radish 121 □ Squash 122 □ Sweet-corn 124 □ Swiss chard 125 □ Tomato 126 □ Turnip 129 □ Watermelon 130 □
11. LESSER GROWN AND KNOWN VEGETABLES 131
    Artichoke, globe, Jerusalem 131 □ Asparagus 132 □ Cabbage, Chinese, 133 □ Celery 133 □ Celeriac 133 □ Chicory, witloof 134 □ Endive 134 □ Florence fennel 134 □ Garlic 135 □ Horseradish 135 □ Kale 135 □ Kohlrabi 135 □ Mustard spinach 136 □ Okra 136 □ Onion types 137 □ Rhubarb 137 □ Salsify 138 □ Spinach 138 □ Swede 138 □ Sweet potato 138 □ Watercress 139 □
12. PESTS AND DISEASES 140

Glossary 150
Index 156

Preface

This book breaks new ground and brings together for the first time — translated into home-garden application and backed by experimental work conducted by the author in his experimental–demonstration vegetable garden — results of much recent research into vegetable production.

The material has been put into concise and readable form which makes this book an invaluable, speedy reference for vegetable gardeners.

Many aspects of gardening have changed in recent years, the most dramatic being vegetable gardening with the realisation that a vegetable garden decreases the cost of food, provides a satisfying, profitable and productive use of leisure time, is creative, therapeutic and educational, and gives the gardener a sense of achievement rarely emulated by any other form of gardening.

Above all, vegetable gardening is the means of providing the home with inflation-free, tax-free, home-grown produce — healthier, fresher and tastier than from any other source.

CAPEL HEMY
Howick, 1984

1
Planning

Planning is the first and basic operation in growing vegetables. Planning saves time, labour, money and avoids waste. It also provides an estimate of the seeds or plants and cultivars needed, but, most importantly, helps to ensure a supply of vegetables throughout the year.

When planning the season's programme, take into account the family's preferences and needs. The aim should be to produce a good range of vegetables that will be enjoyed throughout the year.

Before each planting season a rough 'blueprint' of the vegetable plot should be prepared. Include in the sketch the vegetables to be sown or planted, which rows they will occupy, the distances between and in the rows, expected sowing dates, likely harvesting periods and any other helpful information.

The aim in planning a vegetable garden is to keep it in production for as long as possible. In many areas of Southern Africa it is possible for a vegetable garden to be productive throughout the year. In hot, humid

Good planning will keep production gaps to a minimum. Delays in sowings and plantings often cause breaks in continuity cropping.

GROWING VEGETABLES

areas and those where severe frosts are experienced there will be gaps in production, but good planning will keep them to a minimum.

The days when beds in a vegetable garden were 'rested' have gone. The practice now is to use them to their maximum capacity by replacing the soil's expended energy with bulky manure and compost supplemented with fertilizers. Intensive vegetable gardening succeeds, provided that a high level of soil fertility is maintained.

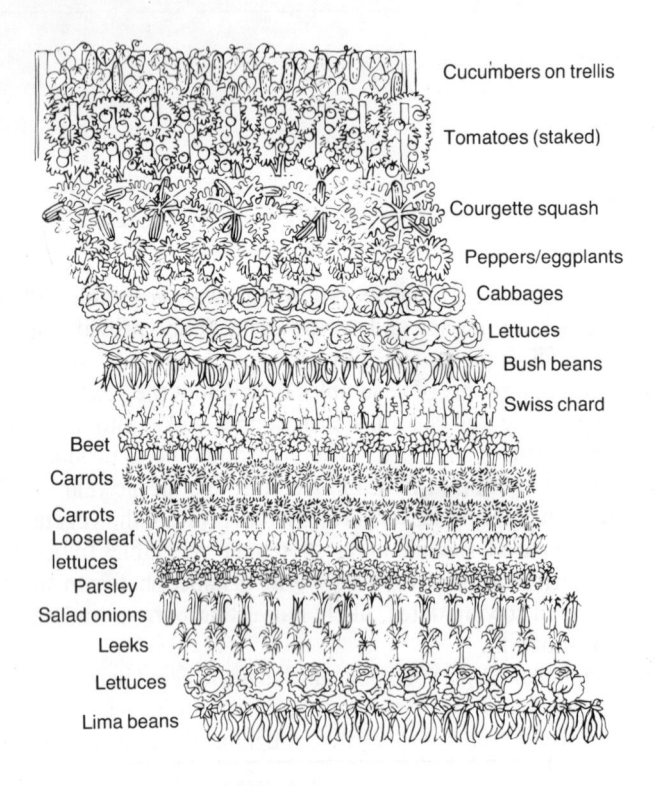

Cucumbers on trellis
Tomatoes (staked)
Courgette squash
Peppers/eggplants
Cabbages
Lettuces
Bush beans
Swiss chard
Beet
Carrots
Carrots
Looseleaf lettuces
Parsley
Salad onions
Leeks
Lettuces
Lima beans

The practice of resting sections of a vegetable garden is unnecessary. The entire plot should be used to its maximum capacity throughout the year by maintaining high soil fertility.

The summer vegetable garden illustrated concentrates most of the long-term vegetables at the top of the plot. Successive sowings should be made of other vegetables, except lima beans, to provide continuity cropping.

A 10 x 5 m plot should be adequate to supply a wide range of summer vegetables with space cleared later for successive sowings and plantings of winter vegetables.

Make notes of when each vegetable is to be sown and the number of sowings of each. Estimate when the crops will be cleared and ensure some beds will be available when needed for early sowings or plantings of the following season's crops.

A critical period in planning, and its implementation, is when the seasons overlap — harvesting of one season's crops and planting of the next. With the intensive-cropping system careful planning is necessary to avoid delays in new bed preparation. Delays may cause breaks in continuity cropping.

When planning a year-round vegetable garden, there are several points to take into account. Avoid small beds with both fast-maturing and long-term vegetables; for example, bush beans and eggplants. A September sowing of bush beans will probably be finished by late December, while an October planting of eggplant may produce fruits through to March or later. New bed preparation would be unnecessarily delayed.

The plan should allow for staggered sowings of fast-growing and short-term harvest vegetables such as lettuce, bush beans, radish, carrot, beet, cabbage and salad onions.

Small, successive sowings will give continuity harvesting, while large, spasmodic sowings will result in surpluses followed by shortages.

Take into account crops with a long growing season and plan accordingly. These include: broad bean, lima bean, Brussels sprouts, celery, some cauliflower cultivars, eggplant, leek, New Zealand spinach, onion, parsnip, pepper, pumpkin, some squash cultivars, Swiss chard and indeterminate tomatoes.

Note the average times between sowing and germination, then add them to the estimated growing period through to the completion of the harvest to get a reasonably accurate idea of when beds will be ready for the following crops.

Planning beds in advance will, after two or three years of recording the location of various vegetable cultivars, simplify crop rotation. Good crop rotation should ensure that each crop makes optimum use of the soil and existing fertility as well as avoiding the possibility of a build up of soil pests and diseases specifically relating to a particular vegetable.

When planning, the size of the vegetable garden must be considered. The smaller the plot the more necessary it will be to concentrate on crops where freshness is of major importance — for example, lettuce, radish, carrot, bush bean, salad onion and tomato.

A well-managed small plot will equal the yield of a badly managed large one, and with much less effort.

It takes at least two hours a week to maintain a 15 by 5 m area, not including sowing or planting and harvesting.

Once the plan of the vegetable garden is prepared it is necessary to keep records of the crops grown. Recording work done in the vegetable garden is sound economy. Records may show some vegetables not to be worth growing because they take up too much space, are in the ground too long and for the yields they produce and so on.

A well-bound, hardcover book with ruled pages and big enough to make adequate notes should be used for recording. At the top of the pages write the name of each vegetable to be grown, leaving several pages for each. Also leave spare pages for vegetables which may be introduced at a later stage.

If the vegetable garden is to be divided into separate beds, draw a plan of each bed and indicate the manure, compost and fertilizers to be used. The sketch should also show where the vegetables are sown or planted each season to help with crop rotation and show how the bed can be used to maximum capacity.

Do not rely on memory. It is important to learn and record as much as possible about the garden's environment, the performances of plants, optimum sowing and planting times, responses to fertilizer applications, pest and disease problems, growing times, yields and any other points that will make planning easier in later seasons.

A maximum/minimum thermometer and a rain gauge in close proximity to the vegetable garden can supply much valuable information, particularly after records have been kept for a few years. It is often possible to predict fairly accurately when the first frost is due and show the periods when supplementary irrigation will be necessary.

Here is a typical entry that may appear in the record book under the heading of 'Bush Bean':

August 25. Seminole sown in 450 mm rows, 100 mm apart in the row. No germination.

September 15. Repeat sowing, harvesting commenced November 20 (66 days), harvesting completed December 21. Yield 1,8 kg/1 m row.

September 30. Seminole sown in 450 mm rows, 50 mm apart in the row. Harvesting commenced November 30 (61 days), harvesting completed December 30. Yield 2,5 kg/1 m row.

The information indicates the soil was too cold for germination in August and the closer within-row spacing of the September 30 sowing resulted in a higher yield.

It takes a year or two to compile records of real benefit, but once available they are invaluable for forward planning.

2
Site and Climate

Climate and siting are important for successful vegetable growing. In urban areas the choice of a vegetable site is often limited by the position of the house, neighbouring trees, walls, fences and other factors influencing the amount of sun the site receives.

It then becomes an exercise in compromise, where site-imposed restrictions mean finding the best area available. It may be better to look for two sites, one for summer and another for winter when shadows are more pronounced.

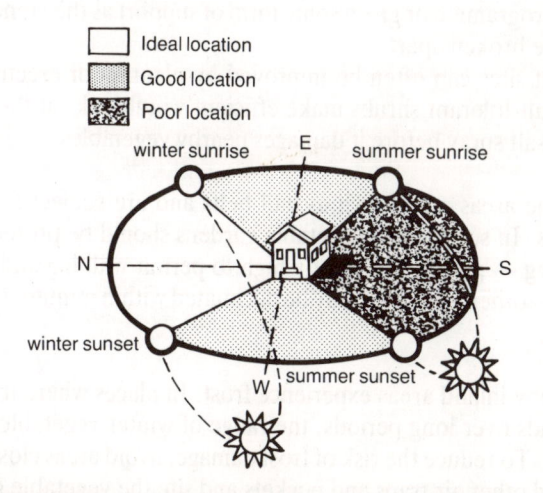

Plan the vegetable garden so that it gets maximum sun. A southern aspect is not recommended, particularly during the winter months, as long shadows are often cast by buildings, trees and other structures.

Vegetables prefer full sun, but many can be grown with a minimum of about six hours daily. There are no shade-loving vegetables.

If there is a choice of aspect, a north-east facing one is preferable. It receives early morning sun when warmth is needed and may give some protection from cold, prevailing winds from the south in winter and hot afternoon sun in summer.

Shade cast by tall trees with few lower branches can be beneficial as shade moves with the sun and usually provides filtered rather than dense shade. Trees too close to a vegetable garden can, however, take up much of the available nutrients and moisture and their root systems often extend beyond the distance between trunk and outer branches.

Whether rows should run north to south or east to west is of relative unimportance in Southern Africa as the sun is sufficiently high to avoid causing excessive plant shading, even in winter. Therefore, the direction of rows need not be a limiting factor when planning beds.

Water: The availability of water is an important consideration when choosing the site. No vegetable garden can be totally dependent on rain, so that alternative sources must be available when sowing, transplanting and during dry periods. Ideally, a tap or rainwater tank should be close by.

Wind: In very windy areas, often at the coast, tall-growing vegetables such as pole beans and sweet-corn may either have to be left out of the growing programme or given some form of support as they tend to blow over or are broken apart.

Difficult sites can often be improved by planting or erecting windbreaks. Salt-tolerant shrubs make efficient windbreaks at the coast as they trap salt spray before it damages nearby vegetables.

Hail: Some areas are known as hail belts and are subject to summer hailstorms. In such areas, vegetable gardens should be protected with hail netting — placed sufficiently high to permit walking and working beneath — otherwise crops may be decimated within minutes of a storm breaking.

Frost: Many inland areas experience frost. In places where it is severe and extends over long periods, the range of winter vegetables may be restricted. To reduce the risk of frost damage, avoid areas close to solid fences and other air traps and pockets and site the vegetable garden at the top half of a slope.

Solid windbreaks should be avoided as frost flow may be impeded and build up, causing damage to nearby plants. If there is an adequate air flow, the risk of damage should be reduced.

Sloping ground: A vegetable garden established on sloping ground needs more preparation and attention than one on the flat. The biggest problem is soil erosion and the best solution is to terrace the area, preferably with 1,2 to 1,5 m wide beds across the slope with narrow paths between. Bed levels must always be maintained, particularly during the rainfall season.

Climate: It is possible only to generalise here because of the wide-ranging climatic variations in all regions.

Unless accurate climatic records are available, information should be sought from local gardeners, nurserymen and others who can give sound information until personal records are more comprehensive.

Climatic factors of concern to gardeners are: temperature, rainfall, sun, wind and frost. All can influence a growing season although the climatic tolerance of a specific vegetable also plays a role. Many vegetables tolerate cold down to freezing point and below although they may not grow actively at low temperatures.

Climate is often important to the quality of produce. Under high temperatures ripening is accelerated and quality reduced. The sugar content of some vegetables increases when the weather is clear and mild with cool night temperatures.

Extended periods of warm, wet weather often produce vegetables with a low sugar content, which are watery and sometimes soft and flabby. These conditions are also conducive to a build up of pests and diseases.

Because climate varies considerably within any region, it is not possible to oversimplify recommendations. In the following brief descriptions of the six climatic regions of South Africa only basic information is, therefore, given. See also the map of the six regions overleaf.

Vegetables are grown at altitudes between sea level and in excess of 2 000 m so that a wide range of growing conditions could be expected: in fact, there are relatively few. The major exceptions are in areas where severe and extended frosts occur, extremes of heat in lowveld and arid areas, and a combination of heat and humidity along the Natal seaboard and adjacent interior.

Region 1. The Western Cape is generally characterised by a cool, sometimes cold, wet winter with warm and dry, hot summers. The main rainfall period is between May and September. Because of the divergence of geographical features, average rainfall varies between 200 mm and more than 3 000 mm.

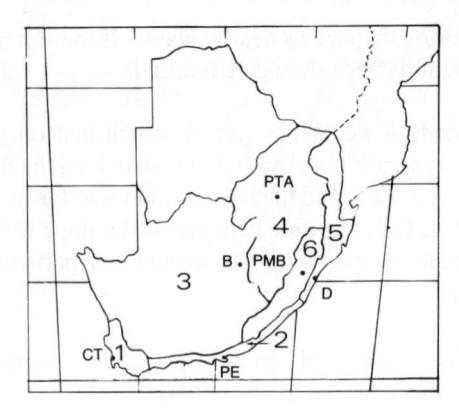

Frost can occur on higher ground, but is unusual along the coast. Hail is a rare occurrence.

In summer there are usually strong south-east winds that restrict the growing of some tall-growing vegetables without windbreaks. Strong, north-west winds usually prevail in winter.

A full range of vegetables may be grown in this region and, with few exceptions, have sowing and planting times similar to those in most other regions.

Region 2. The western section of this coastal belt region is, in some respects, similar to region 1 as it can have winter rainfall. Most of this section has both winter and summer rainfall, although autumn and spring rains are usually more dependable.

In the eastern section summer rainfall can be expected, although there may be limited winter rains.

The climate is temperate along the seaboard and cooler with lower humidity further inland. Rainfall in the west averages between 400 and 1 100 mm while the average varies between 500 and 1 250 mm in the eastern section.

Frost may occur on high ground, but is usually of short duration and not severe. Hail is rare in the west of the region, but may accompany thunderstorms in the eastern section.

Strong coastal winds are experienced throughout most of the year.

Most vegetables may be grown in season, and in the warmer coastal areas of the eastern section some of the hardier 'summer' vegetables may be grown during winter.

Region 3. A vast area which ranges between arid and semi-arid. Summers are hot, often with cool nights and large day-night temperature fluctuations. Winter frosts are usually severe and in some areas extend over several months.

Rainfall is unreliable, ranging from 500 mm a year in the east to 250 mm in the central area and less than 50 mm near the west coast. Summer and autumn are the main periods for rain. Limited winter rain is possible near the west coast.

Severe frosts are common in all inland areas. Hail is possible in summer in the eastern half of the region. Strong winds are experienced along the west coast throughout the year.

Subject to water availability, most summer crops may be grown. In winter only the hardiest vegetables should be grown.

Region 4. The lower section of this region (highveld) has summer rainfall with cool to cold winters. Some parts of the higher section have very hot summers with summer rainfall and mild winters. Rainfall can be expected between September and March, often peaking in January. The lower section of the region averages between 650 to 900 mm a year, while the northern area has an average between 380 mm in the far north to 700 mm further south.

The climate in the far north is semi-arid and very hot in summer with cool to cold winters. In the lower areas summers are hot with cool to cold winters.

Frosts are frequent between May and September in the lower section. Parts of the higher section are generally frost-free although frosts do occur in the non-lowveld areas. Frequent summer hailstorms can be expected in the lower part of the region.

A full range of seasonal vegetables may be grown throughout most of the region. In the northern section of the lowveld area summer production may be difficult and 'summer' vegetables are frequently grown during winter.

Region 5. This region includes coastal Natal, adjacent interiors and the eastern Transvaal lowveld. Most of the region is referred to as subtropical, although frosts do occur in some areas.

Summer rainfall occurs between October and March with a peak in January. The coastal belt may also have some winter rain. In the lower section of the region rainfall varies between 750 mm in the interior to about 1 250 mm along the coast. In the north the average annual rainfall is between 500 and 700 mm but may rise to 2 000 mm along the escarpment.

GROWING VEGETABLES

In the north the summer climate is warm to hot with some humidity. The coastal belt is warm to hot and humid with lower humidity in the adjacent interior.

Light frost may be experienced inland from the coastal belt. In higher areas of the lowveld frosts may occur between May and September. Hail is a summer hazard in some lowveld areas.

Growing vegetables in summer can be problematical in coastal and lowveld areas because of heat and humidity and their attendant diseases. 'Summer' vegetables are usually grown in winter in frost-free areas.

Region 6. This region has a variable climate ranging from relatively frost-free towards region 5 to parts where severe frosts are experienced. The influence of altitude and the Drakensberg range are mainly responsible for the fluctuations in the region.

Rainfall mainly occurs in summer between October and March. Light winter rains are possible in some areas. Rainfall varies between 650 mm on lower ground to 1 900 mm near the Drakensberg.

Climate is warm to hot in summer with cool to cold — sometimes very cold — winters, depending on altitude. Frosts occur between April and September. Hailstorms can be expected over wide areas in summer.

A full range of summer and winter vegetables may be grown in most parts of the region. In the coldest areas only the hardiest winter vegetables are usually successful.

3
Soil Management

Soil is usually taken for granted as being a medium which, given some organic matter, fertilizer and water, will produce vegetables. Good soil management, however, plays an important role in growing good quality vegetables.

The function of soil is to give support and anchorage to plants; it must supply water, oxygen and nutrients needed for plant growth, be relatively free of toxic elements such as soil-borne pests and diseases, harmful bacteria and fungi, and permit plants to produce vigorous, healthy and unrestricted root systems.

Given these basics, most vegetables grow in soils ranging from light sandy soil through to heavy clay if the soil is well drained, has high fertility and a soil acidity–alkalinity range reasonably correct for each vegetable.

Generally, gardeners have little choice in positioning a vegetable garden, and when once established many sites are not changed for years, if ever. Even with good rotation the possibilities of build-ups of soil pests and diseases are always present and may make vegetable growing more difficult.

Most soils contain varying percentages of organic matter, called humus. This is a material formed by partial decomposition of organic matter in or on the soil. Its main functions are to release plant nutrients as it is being broken down by soil bacteria and to bind soil particles which makes the soil more efficient for plant development.

The importance of organic matter in the soil cannot be overemphasised. Almost all soils can support plant life if organic matter in the form of animal manure, compost, decomposed leaves, grass clippings, straw, hay and other similar materials is added. Dark-brown

GROWING VEGETABLES

soils usually indicate a high organic matter content with the topsoil containing the highest percentage.

Organic matter is not only a stabilising factor in soil texture and a source of limited plant nutrients, it is also a soil conditioner. It increases the soil's capacity to hold moisture and nutrients, it lightens heavy soils, adds body to light soils and helps reduce soil crusting, which often retards seedling emergence.

Some indications of poor soils are: misshapen root vegetables, poor and shallow root systems, low yields, rapid and regular wilting in dry weather, crusting of the soil surface, poor drainage and an inability to dig to a full spade's depth.

One of the common problems encountered in Southern Africa is the 'hard-pan' — a solid layer immediately below the topsoil. Hard-pans are often the result of frequent shallow cultivation and result in stunting and low yields.

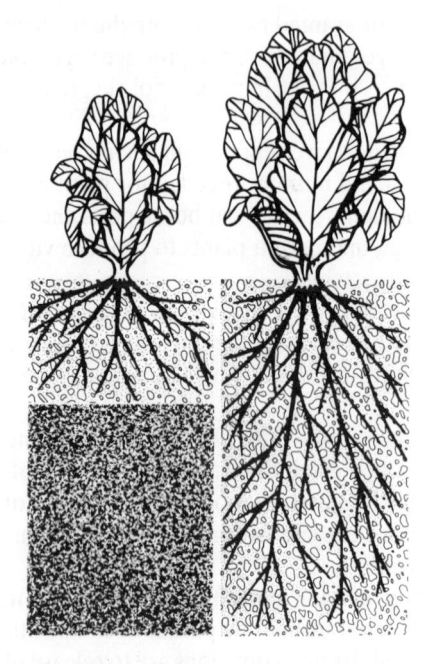

A hard-pan is a solid layer just below the topsoil and is the result of shallow cultivation. A hard-pan restricts root growth, causing stunting and lower yields.

If it is established that poor plant growth is not due to poor physical condition of the soil, lack of water or too much of it, low soil temperatures, soil pests and diseases, or poorly germinating seeds, then the

SOIL MANAGEMENT

most likely reason is malnutrition, which a soil test should show.

Whether or not a soil test is made, the object should be to build up soil fertility as quickly as possible. The use of organic matter alone to build up fertility is not usually practical as vast amounts would be needed: the nutrient content of most organic matter is low.

The minimum requirement of organic matter to maintain or increase the humus level in the soil is about 6 kg/m^2 annually and double the amount is needed for intensive production. Even this quantity would not supply plants with their total nutrient requirements.

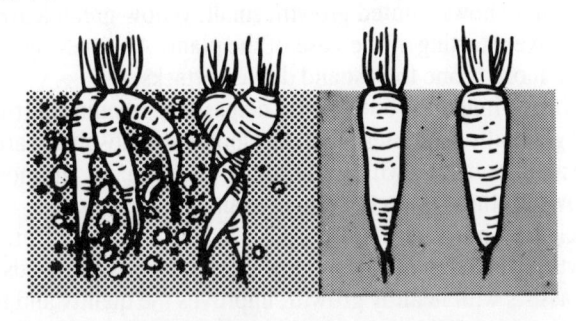

Misshapen root vegetables are often caused by poor soil, irregular watering or a hard-pan beneath a shallow topsoil. Good soils produce good roots.

Fertilizers are chemical (inorganic) manures containing plant foods in a concentrated, easily soluble form that is quickly absorbed by the roots. Results from the application of some fertilizers may be dramatic, but they should not be used to the exclusion of organic matter as this could lead to the breakdown of the soil structure, which, in turn, will lead to poor results regardless of the quantities of fertilizer used.

Soil maintenance, for optimum growth, is a combination of using organic matter at least once a year — more often with intensive growing — to ensure adequate humus for good soil structure, plus fertilizers for specific plants' needs before sowing or planting and as a supplementary feed during the growing period.

Nitrogen, phosphorus and potash (NPK) are the plant foods most likely to be lacking in the soil. They can be used individually if the soil is known to be deficient in any one. A soil analysis is required, however, accurately to determine the specific deficiency.

For this reason, blended (compound) fertilizers are more frequently used. The value of a blended fertilizer is measured by the availability of each nutrients to plants. In South Africa these values are given as a percentage of total plant food.

For example: A 20 kg bag of 2:3:4(24) fertilizer contains 24 per cent plant food (4,8 kg) in the NPK ratio. In this mixture the total plant food is divided into nine parts — 2+3+4 = 2/9N, 3/9P and 4/9K.

Nitrogen is the main nutrient required by plants. It is necessary for good growth and leaf colour. Leaf vegetables such as cabbage, Brussels sprouts and kale are heavy users of nitrogen. It gives the dark-green colour to plants, promotes leaf, stem, fruit and seed growth and helps to break down organic matter in the soil.

Almost all vegetables benefit from supplementary nitrogen feeding during the growing period.

A deficiency shows stunted growth, small, yellow-green leaves, and drying of leaves starting at the base of the plant. An excess gives lush, soft growth more prone to pest and disease attacks.

Phosphorus stimulates root growth, helps in the ripening of fruits and seeds and generally promotes plant development. Phosphates are more readily available in soils with a pH range of 5,5 to 7,5. In more acid soils, below 5,5, there is a reduction in availability.

A deficiency shows through purplish leaves, stems and branches, slow growth, delayed maturity and low yields of fruits and seeds.

Potash assists with healthy growth, improves the quality and texture of most vegetables and helps to build up disease resistance. Most root vegetables respond to a high level of potash.

The main signs of potash deficiency are mottling, spotting, streaking or curling of leaves, browning or scorching of leaf tips, premature leaf loss and growth restriction.

In addition to the three major elements — NPK — there are others needed by plants for healthy vigorous growth but in much smaller quantities, usually referred to as minor or trace elements.

These are: calcium, mainly used to correct acid and toxic soil conditions; magnesium, which helps in chlorophyll formation (green leaf colouring); and sulphur for general plant health. Iron, manganese, boron, zinc, copper and molybdenum are needed by plants only in trace amounts, but unless available various deficiency symptoms may occur.

A trace element mixture, containing these elements and used according to instruction, should soon regulate plants' growth where trace element deficiencies are observed.

There are a number of fertilizer blends available in garden packs, including: 2:3:2(22), 2:3:2(22)Zn (includes the zinc trace element), 2:3:4(24), 3:1:5(31), 3:2:1(25), 4:1:1(33), 5:1:5. This last one is a 'slow-release' fertilizer, releasing nitrogen over a longer period than conventional blended fertilizers. There are other blends available in larger packs.

Superphosphate should be used when beds are dug to ensure that there are sufficient phosphates in the soil to feed plants through a season or possibly a year.

LAN (limestone ammonium nitrate) is a straight nitrogen fertilizer used for supplementary feeding during active plant growth. Nitrogen is the one nutrient quickly used up or leached from the soil.

How much fertilizer to apply? Without a soil analysis no accurate forecast of quantities required can be made. Also, different vegetables have varying requirements. As few gardeners have their soils analysed, a compromise must be reached whereby an approximate rate of application will suit a wide range of vegetables.

In the chapter on 'The Basic Vegetables', a basic fertilizer programme is given based on superphosphate for bed preparation, 2:3:2 or 2:3:4 as planting mixtures, and LAN as a supplementary nitrogen sidedressing.

Soil pH: Most vegetables grow well in slightly to moderately acid soils so it is important to know the degree of soil acidity or alkalinity.

The basis for determining it is the pH scale. The scale runs from 0 to 14 with its centre at pH 7,0, which indicates a neutral soil. A higher value, pH 7,5, indicates a slightly alkaline soil, while pH 6,5 is slightly acid. A difference of one point on the scale indicates a multiplication of 10 times so a pH of 5,5 is 10 times more acid than a pH of 6,5.

Inexpensive, simple to operate and understand, pH kits are available and should be part of every vegetable gardener's equipment.

Alkalinity can be reduced by about 0,5 of a unit by digging in 500 g ammonium sulphate to 10 m^2. Agricultural lime will reduce acidity, using 300 g/m^2 on light soils to raise the pH by about one unit and double the amount on heavy soils.

Reducing acidity by raising the pH must be done gradually. Too heavy applications of lime can result in a soil reaction 'locking up' some soil nutrients and making them unavailable to plants' roots. Nutrients most affected are phosphates, potassium (potash), magnesium, manganese and boron.

Correct liming of an acid soil helps to release potassium, magnesium, molybdenum and other plant foods that may not have been available because of excess acidity.

More problems are created by overliming than underliming, however. Because most vegetables prefer slighty acid soil conditions, be sure that lime is necessary before applying.

pH preferences: Slightly acid (6,0 to 7,0) — asparagus, beet, broad bean, broccoli, cabbage, carrot, cauliflower, celery, Chinese cabbage, leek, lettuce, lima bean, melon, New Zealand spinach, okra, onion, parsley, parsnip, pumpkin, spinach, squash, Swiss chard, radish and watercress.

Moderately acid (5,5 to 6,5) — bean bush and pole, Brussels sprouts, cucumber, eggplant, garlic, horseradish, pepper, sweet-corn, tomato and turnip.

Acid (5,0 to 6,0) — chicory, endive, potato, rhubarb, sweet potato and watermelon.

ROTATION

Crop rotation is important, particularly when a vegetable garden is used intensively. The rigid division of the vegetable garden into three or four sections, commonly advocated for the purposes of rotation, has little application in modern intensive culture, mainly because limited space and full use of beds throughout most of the year preclude the operation of old rotation systems. With careful planning a more acceptable form of rotation can be devised.

If one vegetable is grown continuously in the same position, some pests and diseases such as nematodes (eelworm) and wilts will build up in the soil.

The two important points to consider in modern rotation are:
- Never grow the same, or a related crop in the same place two years in succession.
- Never grow vegetables with extensive root systems in succession.

Bearing these points in mind, it is possible to work out a basic system of rotation. There are a few 'grey' areas where it is thought that crops with different root systems may give unsatisfactory yields, but if the correct soil fertility is provided for specific crops this problem should be overcome.

Related crops with large root systems:
Brassicas: broccoli, Brussels sprouts, cabbage, cauliflower, kale.
   (Kohlrabi, radish and turnip are listed under root vegetables.)
Tomato family: eggplant, pepper, potato and tomato.
Legumes: bush, lima, pole and broad beans and peas.
Maize family: sweet-corn.
Cucurbits: cucumber, melon, pumpkin, squash and watermelon.

Related crops with medium root systems:
Lettuce family: chicory, endive, lettuce and salsify.
Parsley family: celery, celeriac and parsley. (Carrot and parsnip are
   listed under root vegetables.)

SOIL MANAGEMENT

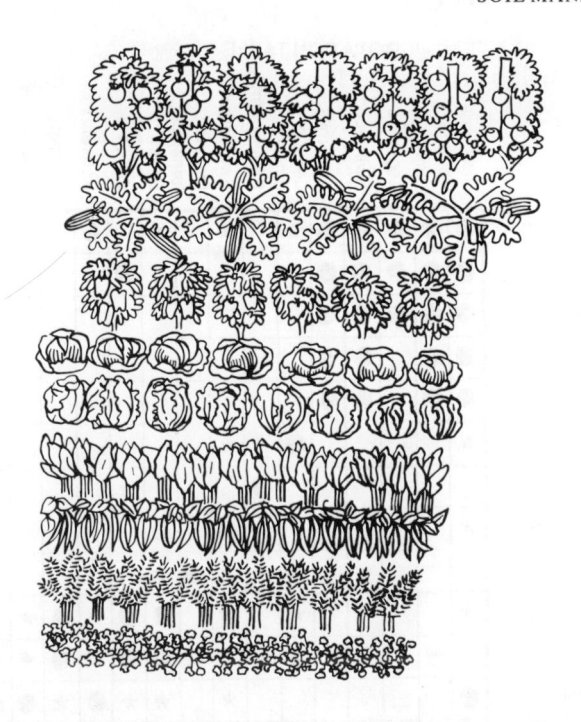

Two major points to remember in modern rotation: never grow the same or related vegetables in the same place two years in succession, and avoid successional sowings or plantings of vegetables with extensive root systems.

At the top of the illustration tomatoes, squash and peppers — all with extensive root systems — are kept together. In the following year they would be moved down the plot, replacing lettuce, beet, bush beans, carrot and parsley.

Beet family: Swiss chard — New Zealand spinach is not related. (Beet is listed under root vegetables.)
Onion family: garlic, leek, onion.
Root vegetables: beet, carrot, kohlrabi, parsnip, radish, turnip.

When growing brassicas, members of the tomato family and cucurbits, try to avoid using the same soil for three years.

The outdated rotational recommendations of applying organic matter the first year, followed by fertilizers in the second and third years of a three-year rotation, should not be followed as they will lead to a decline in soil fertility and lower the humus level.

Experiments have shown that the addition of recommended quantities of *well-rotted* manure or compost does *not* cause misshapen roots of carrots, parsnips and other root vegetables. It invariably gives better

GROWING VEGETABLES

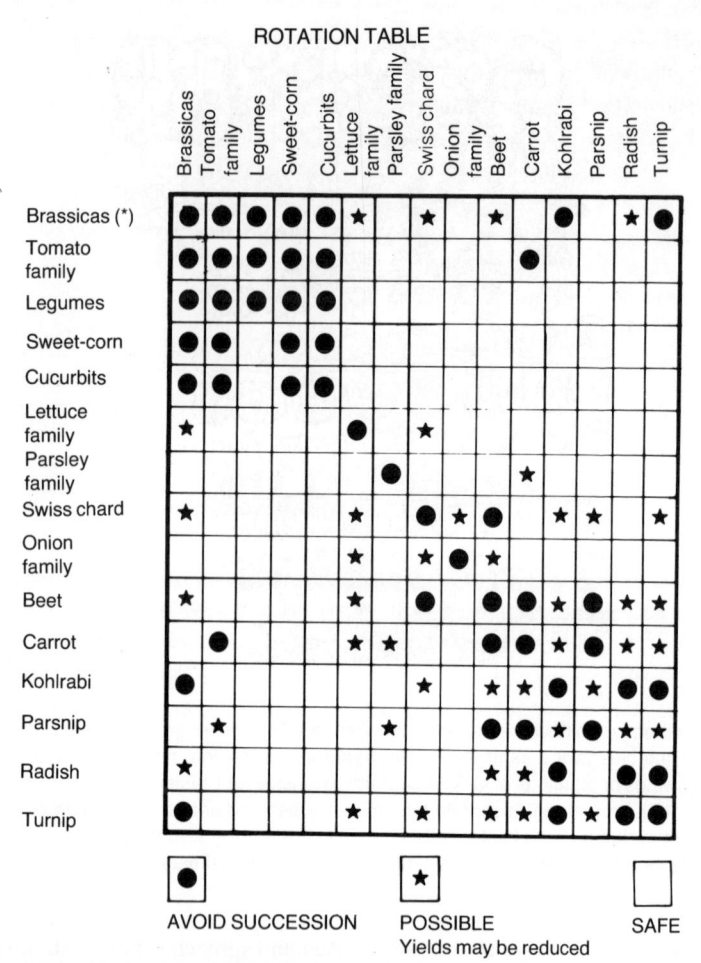

ROTATION TABLE

Previous crop ↓ / Next crop →	Brassicas	Tomato family	Legumes	Sweet-corn	Cucurbits	Lettuce family	Parsley family	Swiss chard	Onion family	Beet	Carrot	Kohlrabi	Parsnip	Radish	Turnip
Brassicas (*)	●	●	●	●	●	★		★		●				★	●
Tomato family	●	●	●	●	●				●						
Legumes	●	●	●	●	●										
Sweet-corn	●	●		●	●										
Cucurbits	●	●		●	●										
Lettuce family	★					●		★							
Parsley family							●			★					
Swiss chard	★					★		●	★	●		★	★		★
Onion family						★		★	●	★					
Beet	★					★		●		●	●	★	●	★	★
Carrot		●				★	★			●	●	★	●	★	★
Kohlrabi	●							★		★	★	●	★	●	●
Parsnip		★					★			●	●	★	●	★	★
Radish	★									★	★	●			●	●
Turnip	●					★		★		★	★	●	★	●	●

● AVOID SUCCESSION   ★ POSSIBLE (Yields may be reduced)   ☐ SAFE

To read the table for successional sowing or planting, select the vegetable to be grown in the vertical column on the left, check along the horizontal line for the previous crop, then note the symbol for rotational suitability.

(*) Excludes related root vegetables which are listed separately.

yields and quality, particularly when grown in deep-beds which maintain a high organic matter content.

FOLIAR FEEDING

Applying nutrients to the leaves should be used as a supplement and not as a substitute for manures and fertilizers from which plants obtain their food through the roots.

Foliar feeds can, however, correct trace element deficiencies more rapidly and effectively than application to the soil. Experiments have shown that plants make use of 90 per cent of feeding materials applied to leaves and only 10 per cent of those placed on soil in the root area.

Foliar feeding can overcome the problem of elements being 'locked' in the soil because of too much lime, or a too acid soil that would otherwise result in poor growth from an imbalance of plant food.

It is also valuable where a plant has grown too fast, as can happen with maturing tomatoes and cucumbers in tunnels and greenhouses, when the root system cannot cope with plant growth and fruit maturity.

Where a root system has been damaged, foliar feeding can provide temporary first-aid until the plant recovers.

A further advantage of foliar feeding is the stimulatory effect it has on a wide range of plants after they have received a set-back, such as frost, hail or drought damage.

Foliar feeds are economical to use, compatible with most pesticides and may be applied with them in one spraying operation.

Experiments conducted on seaweed concentrate foliar feed have shown numerous benefits may be expected, such as: more economical use of plant nutrients, stronger plant growth, heavier yields, longer shelf life of several vegetables, retardation of fungal development, increase in resistance to frost, making some leaves unpalatable to insects, earlier and stronger root development, reduction of transplanting shock and a delay in wilting.

4
Watering

All vegetables need water to survive. Too little will result in low yields and poor quality. Too much will produce similar results.

Not all vegetables need the same amount of water, however, and it is important to know their requirements otherwise both time and effort will be wasted. Overwatering can produce excessive leaf growth in vegetables where the leaf is not the edible portion, restricted root growth and leaching of nitrogen from the soil.

Water requirements also vary with the stage of growth. In the small, emergent-seedling stage frequent light waterings are necessary, a system of watering not recommended for established plants.

Vegetables producing fruits and edible seeds, such as tomatoes, eggplants, peppers, cucumbers, melons, squash, beans, peas and sweetcorn, need more water when they start flowering and as the fruits and seeds develop.

Vegetables grown in light, sandy soils need more water than those in heavier, more water-retentive soils.

Vegetables need an average of 25 mm of rain a week or the equivalent from supplementary irrigation. Translated into hand watering, the equivalent is about 25 litres/m^2. These are arbitrary figures, as an area which has dried out and been left for weeks or months in dry weather may need up to 75 litres/m^2 to moisten soil to the full rooting depth of a crop.

The weather also influences water requirements. In hot, dry, cloudless conditions plants not only need water to take up dissolved nutrients in the soil but also to keep them cool. Under these conditions, water loss through transpiration can be as much as five times higher than under cloudy, cool conditions. This becomes obvious when outdoor temperatures — not in shade — may be in excess of 45°C.

In summer, with hot, dry conditions, transpiration and evaporation could account for 25 mm rain (25 litres/m^2) in four or five days.

WATERING METHODS

These are guidelines only, based on beds with medium amounts of organic matter. Adaptations should be made according to the season and local conditions.

Seedlings: The critical time is between sowing and emergence of the seedling. At all times the soil in contact with the seed must be moist. The period of time will vary according to the kind of vegetable, soil temperature and sowing depth.

Transplants: Watering before and after transplanting is essential, particularly in hot weather when young plants are unable to replace water lost from the leaves as fast as they need because of some inevitable root damage. This condition is known as transplanting shock.

Zone watering: Under some circumstances, such as water restrictions or rationing, it is impossible to maintain a water application of 25 litres/m^2 each week. Zone watering has proved effective in reducing the amount of water used while maintaining good plant growth.

Zone watering — applying water to the immediate root zone — can save water. After sowing or transplanting hills (bowls) made around the seed or plant — as in the illustration — will contain water to the immediate area.

Initially, a bed should be thoroughly moistened to the full rooting depth of the crop to be grown. Thereafter apply water to the immediate root zone using a watering can with or without a rose on the spout, depending on the size of plants.

A good deep watering alongside a row or on either side of a row should maintain adequate soil moisture if supported with a good mulch. Zone watering may be used for most vegetables and has proved particularly effective for root crops such as carrots, beet and parsnips.

Zone watering by hand is also preferable when watering the foliage is to be avoided.

A good deep watering, followed by a deep mulch will help retain soil moisture, regulate soil temperatures, reduce weed growth and save water.

WATER REQUIREMENTS

Leaf crops: Brussels sprouts, cabbage, celery, Chinese cabbage, endive, kale, lettuce, parsley, spinach and Swiss chard plus broccoli, cauliflower and leeks.

Leaf crops generally need about 25 litres/m^2 a week and should be kept actively growing from the time they are sown or transplanted. If they receive any check during the growing period, yields or quality or both may suffer.

In summer it may be preferable to split the water requirements into two applications, but heavier waterings should be given as crops approach maturity. In cooler months a single weekly watering is adequate.

Within the group, cauliflowers are most likely to be affected by a check and a common result is 'buttoning' — plants produce premature, poor quality, tiny heads.

Root crops: The main vegetables in this group are beet, carrot, kohlrabi, onion, parsnip, potato, radish and turnip.

The average weekly water requirement is between 10 and 15 litres/

m^2. More may be needed as the plants approach maturity.

A balance between too much and too little water must be achieved for optimum yields. If root vegetables get too much water, excessive leaf growth may occur at the expense of roots. Too much lush growth increases risks of foliar disease such as alternaria on carrots.

Regular watering must be maintained in the absence of rain and it is most important to ensure that water penetrates deeply into the soil.

To encourage deep rooting of carrots and parsnips, do not water too often in their early stages of growth. Withholding water, to a degree, will force the roots to penetrate the soil in search of moisture and should ensure good quality, full-sized roots when harvested. As roots begin to swell, twice-weekly watering may be needed under hot conditions.

Shallow watering discourages good root development. Irregular watering — allowing the soil to dry out followed by heavy watering — may cause roots such as carrots and parsnips to fork.

Potatoes need additional water when tubers start forming.

Other crops: Basic vegetables in this group are broad, bush, lima and pole beans, cucumber, eggplant, melon, pea, pepper, pumpkin, squash, sweet-corn and tomato.

The average weekly water requirement is 25 litres/m^2 but varies according to the stage of development.

A weekly watering, or an even longer period, should be adequate until plants start flowering. Too much water up to this stage encourages excessive leaf growth.

Bush and pole beans and peas have moderately deep rooting systems. Lima and broad beans have deeper ones. Once plants are well established, they will be able to find moisture and nutrients at lower levels in well-prepared deep soils.

Once bean and pea pods have begun to form, watering every two or three days at the rate of 10 litres/m^2 should provide ideal growing conditions.

A similar watering programme can be used for sweet-corn, but extra care will be needed as it has many near-surface feeding roots. Increase watering when cobs form.

Tomatoes, squash, cucumber, pepper, eggplant and melon may be grown in hills (bowls) for zone watering. Soil is ridged to form a circle with a diameter up to 750 mm. The ridge is higher than the inside of the bowl and should be raised further if the bowl is deeply mulched. The advantage of the hill is that it retains moisture within the root zone, particularly as most of these plants have large root systems which are deep but also with near-surface feeding roots.

GROWING VEGETABLES

All cucurbits need plenty of water throughout their growing life. Once flowering and fruiting begin plants will require even more water, particularly courgette squash as each plant is capable of producing large numbers of fruits. Twice-weekly watering should be adequate.

Eggplants and peppers have moderately deep and large root systems, while the tomato root system may be deeper.

Water requirements are not excessive when plants are young, but as soon as the first fruits are formed they will need more water on a regular basis. Soil should never be allowed to dry out. Blossom-end rot of tomato fruits can be a sign of irregular watering.

If plants are grown in hills and mulched, one deep watering a week should ensure sufficient moisture.

For optimum water use it is necessary to know something of the vegetables' root systems. In some instances a plant's rooting depth may differ from the size of root systems discussed under 'Rotation' in the previous chapter.

Shallow-rooted vegetables: broccoli, Brussels sprouts, cabbage, cauliflower, celery, endive, garlic, leek, lettuce, onion, parsley, potato, radish and sweet-corn.
Medium-depth rooted vegetables: bush and bean pole beans, beet, carrot, cucumber, eggplant, melon, pea, pepper, squash, Swiss chard and turnip.
Deep-rooted vegetables: artichoke-globe, asparagus, lima bean, parsnip, pumpkin, some winter-storage squash, tomato and watermelon.

Water-efficient vegetables: Two factors are involved: the rate of growth and the percentage of edible portion against discarded portion.

Lettuce, endive and Swiss chard are the most water efficient, followed by beet, turnip and salad onion.

Then come the heavy fruiting plants such as tomato, pepper and eggplant, which give a continuous flow of fruits over a long period.

Down the line in efficiency are beans, cabbage, broccoli, Brussels sprouts, cauliflower, carrot and squash. They take longer to mature than leaf vegetables and less than half the plant is eaten. The least water-efficient vegetables are okra, pea and sweet-corn.

Wetter water: Soil-wetting agents change the physical properties of water by reducing the surface tension of water molecules, making them less able to stick together and making water more available to the plant.

Water does not always wet soil efficiently, even when uniformly applied. It may penetrate some soils slowly or follow a path of least resistance through a coarse soil or root zone and cause dry areas, with the result that the soil is not evenly moistened. This can lead to shallow rooting, poor growth and, possibly, the introduction of disease.

A soil-wetting agent also helps to spread soil pesticides and fertilizers more uniformly and with longer-lasting effects, because more efficient watering reduces the risks of fast leaching from plants' root zones.

A good wetting agent acts as a water-holding medium and as soil dries it yields its moisture to the soil to maintain an even moisture balance. It will also drain away excess moisture. The two functions help eliminate stress conditions and diseases associated with too much or too little water. It has been claimed that good wetting agents can reduce watering by 30 to 50 per cent.

The main uses of wetting agents in the vegetable garden are in seed-trays, seedbeds and beds into which new transplants are to be placed. Cost is a limiting factor in treating large areas.

Proprietary brand packs are available. A less expensive, probably less efficient, soil-wetting agent is a biodegradable liquid detergent.

Waste (grey) water: Waste water is water from sinks, baths, showers and washing machines. It does not normally need any chemical or biological treatment before being used to water the garden.

Waste-water recycling should be scaled to suit the garden water requirements. Waste water, in excess of what is immediately needed, should be discarded.

Waste water from a dishwasher should *never* be used on vegetables. Water from the final rinse of a washing machine may, however, be used in limited quantities. Washing-machine detergents with 'softening powders' or 'enzymatic action' often contain sodium-based compounds which may have a detrimental effect on soil and plants, although the content in a final rinse should be minimal.

The safest waste water is bath or shower water. There is little conclusive scientific evidence on the long-term effects on soils after prolonged use of bath water. It has been used in the past with no apparent adverse effects on soils or plants.

A conservative figure is that a square metre of good soil, rich in organic matter, is capable of taking about 25 litres of waste a week. Light sandy soils can take more, but the quantity should be reduced on heavy soils.

In summer the amount applied may be higher when surface evaporation and plant transpiration are at a peak. In winter when evaporation and transpiration are low the use of waste water should be reduced.

It is a good plan to rotate the use of waste water with fresh water in order to leach the soil of possible contaminants. In areas maintained on waste water, apply thick mulches to aid natural decomposition of waste residues.

Excessive use of waste water, which is alkaline, may raise the soil pH to an unsatisfactory level for some of the more acid-preferring vegetables.

Drainage water from a shower, bath or washing machine may contain human pathogens — disease-causing organisms — but any potentially harmful bacteria and viruses will be immobilised by the abundant soil organisms present. Further, it is unlikely that they would be assimilated by plant roots and translocated to the edible portion of food plants.

5
Sowing and Transplanting

Seed sowing in rows, open beds, seedbeds, seedtrays and containers often creates problems: too many seedlings, too few, gaps in rows, dying after emergence, no emergence, not knowing how long it should take between sowing and emergence, and so on.

An understanding of seeds and their individual germination requirements should eliminate most problems, providing that seeds are fresh and viable (live) and are given their minimum requirements of air, moisture and an adequately high soil temperature.

A seed is an embryo plant which is surrounded by a skin and an amount of food sufficient to support it from the time it leaves the dormancy state to its appearance above ground.

If the right soil conditions are available and the seed is viable, moisture seeps through the seed coat, starts to dissolve the food and the germination process begins.

The plant embryo first of all pushes out a root and a shoot follows, which grows up towards the soil surface. If the shoot has a long way to travel, the food supply may be exhausted before it reaches the surface and the seedling will die. If the embryo plant is too close to the surface and the surface soil dries out and becomes too hot, the shoot may be killed before it can emerge. It is therefore vital to sow seeds at the correct depth.

As the shoot reaches the surface it produces one or two seed leaves (monocotyledon or dicotyledons). These are primarily food stores, not true leaves, which support the young plant until the first true leaves appear.

The stage between sowing and the appearance of true leaves is a critical one and many seedlings are lost during this period if conditions are not almost perfect.

One of the main reasons seeds fail to grow has been described, but there are other factors influencing germination: the age of the seed, how it has been stored and the temperature and humidity to which it has been subjected.

It is not normally good practice to hold seeds over from one year to the next unless ideal storage conditions have been provided. Seeds in sealed foil packs have a longer life than those in paper packets, but once the seal is broken the seed is subject to conditions similar to those in paper packets.

High temperatures and humidity rapidly speed the life process of seeds. Under such conditions seeds may lose viability in weeks or months. Seeds remain viable longer when stored in dry, cool conditions.

Short-lived seeds — about a year — include: leek, okra, onion, parsley, pepper and parsnip (less than a year). Frequently, lettuce can be included in this group.

Longer-lived seeds are: asparagus, beans, broccoli, Brussels sprouts, cabbage, carrot, cauliflower, celery, eggplant, kale, kohlrabi, New Zealand spinach and turnip.

Those with an even longer life include: cucurbits, endive, radish, Swiss chard and tomato.

If seed is stored from one year to the next, a germination test, made before the sowing season, will indicate the seed viability and save delays in the event of poor germination, which would result in buying a new supply of seed.

Soil crusting (capping) is a common cause of seed failure. If soils are heavily watered after sowing and allowed to dry out, a crust may form. Some soils are more prone to crusting than others.

This bean seedling was damaged by pushing through a crusted soil. Although there are leaves, the growing point has been broken off. Soil should be constantly moist between sowing and germination.

SOWING AND TRANSPLANTING

One way to avoid crusting is to moisten the rows prior to sowing and not water again until germination takes place. Obviously, this would not be possible in hot weather or with seeds needing a long period in which to sprout. Filling the sown rows with moist sand, peat or vermiculite helps, but all three tend to dry out quickly unless regularly watered. Rows may also be covered with mulch, newspaper or plastic sheeting, all of which must be removed at the first sign of germination to admit light.

Seed drills lined and covered with sand or vermiculite overcome the crusting problem, but both must be watered regularly as they dry out quickly in full sun.

From top: Make a shallow drill with a hoe, then water thoroughly before sowing. Sow seeds evenly and thinly, then cover. Finally firm the soil with the back of a rake to ensure good contact between seed and soil.

Light watering with a fine-rosed watering-can does not normally cause soils to crust if they are kept uniformly moist.

Inadequate contact between seed and soil may also be a reason for poor germination and is associated with poor seedbed preparation. As has already been shown, incorrect sowing depth can also influence germination.

Not all seeds need the same moisture and temperature for germination. Vegetables can germinate in soils ranging from slightly moist to very moist. Those that germinate in slightly moist soils are: brassicas, eggplant, pepper, sweet-corn and watermelon.

GROWING VEGETABLES

Vegetables needing more soil moisture are: beans, carrot, cucurbits, leek, melon, New Zealand spinach, spinach, parsley, parsnip, radish, tomato and turnip. Peas, beet, lettuce and Swiss chard need high soil moisture.

SOIL TEMPERATURES FOR GERMINATION

CROP	MINIMUM °C	OPTIMUM RANGE °C	OPTIMUM °C	NUMBER OF DAYS TO GERMI- NATION	MAXIMUM °C
Asparagus	10	15–30	25	10–24	35
Bean, broad	5	10–25	15	10–20	30
Bean, bush	15	15–30	30	6–12	35
Bean, pole	18	18–30	30	6–12	35
Bean, lima	20	20–30	30	7–18	30
Beet	5	10–30	30	6–20	35
Broccoli	5	15–30	30	5–10	35
Brussels sprouts	5	15–30	30	5–10	35
Cabbage	5	15–30	30	4–10	35
Carrot	5	10–30	28	6–15	35
Cauliflower	5	15–30	25	5–10	37
Celery	5	15–20	20	7–14	20
Cucumber	15	20–35	30	3–7	40
Eggplant	20	25–30	30	5–10	30
Kale (Borecole)	5	15–30	30	5–10	35
Kohlrabi	10	10–35	25	1–5	40
Leek	2	15–30	25	4–8	35
Lettuce	2	10–30	25	2–7	30
Melon	15	20–35	25	3–10	35
New Zealand spinach	10	15–30	25	7–20	35
Onion	2	15–30	25	4–8	35
Parsley	10	15–30	30	12–20	30
Parsnip	5	15–25	20	15–20	30
Pea	5	15–30	25	5–10	30
Pepper	15	25–35	25	8–10	35
Pumpkin	15	20–35	35	3–8	40
Radish	5	15–30	30	2–7	35
Spinach	2	15–30	25	5–8	30
Squash	15	20–35	35	3–8	40
Sweet-corn	10	20–35	35	3–8	35
Swiss chard	5	15–30	30	6–15	35
Tomato	10	20–35	30	6–10	35
Turnip	10	10–40	25	1–5	40
Watermelon	15	25–35	30	3–7	35

The number of days to germination is based on sowings made within the optimum soil temperature range. Soil temperatures below and above the optimum range influence germination considerably. Seed sown in soils below the minimum and above the maximum is unlikely to germinate.

SOWING AND TRANSPLANTING

Soil temperatures at sowing times can influence the success or otherwise of successional sowings. It is important to sow seeds within an optimum temperature range: germination will then take place in the shortest time and is predictable to within a few days.

SOWING OR TRANSPLANTING
Some vegetables are direct-seeded, that is, sown where they are to mature. Others give better results when transplanted and some may be direct-seeded or transplanted.

Direct-seeded: Broad, bush, lima and pole beans, beet*, cabbage*, Chinese cabbage, carrot, chicory*, cucumber, endive, kale*, kohlrabi, leek*, lettuce*, melon, New Zealand spinach*, onion*, okra, parsley*, parsnip, pea, pumpkin, radish, spinach, squash, sweet-corn, Swiss chard*, turnip. (* *see also* Direct or transplant.)

Transplant: Asparagus, broccoli, Brussels sprouts, cauliflower, celery, eggplant, globe artichoke, pepper, tomato.

Direct or transplant: Beet (preferably direct-seeded as roots may be damaged), cabbage (transplanting preferred), chicory (direct-seeded but transplanted for winter forcing), kale, leek, lettuce (normally direct-seeded in hot weather unless raised in individual cell seed trays), New Zealand spinach, onion, parsley, Swiss chard. Cucurbits may be started in planting bags, but if root development is even slightly checked yields may be reduced; transplanting is not normally recommended.

SEEDBEDS
Seedbeds are for either direct-seeded vegetables or ones in which transplants are raised. Soil preparation is the same: the beds are dug to at least a full spade's depth, organic matter and fertilizers are added. Short-term beds for transplants need less organic matter and fertilizers because the aim is to produce hardy plants. Too lush plants will suffer a set-back when transplanted.

Beds should be prepared in advance of sowing so they can be watered to encourage weed seed germination. Preweeded beds save labour later.

Beds should then be shallowly forked to a depth of about 150 mm and all stones and hard soil clods removed. As most seeds are small, the soil should be raked to a fine tilth (texture), totally free of lumps. A too-fine texture should be avoided as it may cause crusting. Never rake a soil until it becomes a fine dust.

After the bed has been prepared, a light firming may be needed on light soils to reduce air content. Alternatively, rows can be firmed after sowing.

GROWING VEGETABLES

Don't compact the roots into a tight ball. Roots should be gently firmed.

When sowing beds for transplants, use rows 100 to 150 mm apart to facilitate weeding, provide sufficient space and avoid the risk of mixing cultivars.

For the best stands of direct-seeded vegetables or seedbed transplants, seed should be thinly sown to avoid unnecessary or excessive thinning which may damage the roots of remaining plants.

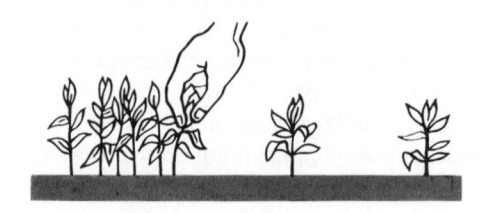

Thinning should be done as early as possible to reduce damage to the roots of remaining plants. If direct-seeded sowings are too thick, thin as soon as possible to recommended within-row spacings.

After seedling emergence, light, frequent waterings are needed to ensure the top 100 mm does not dry out. When seedlings are growing well, the frequency of watering should gradually be reduced to a daily watering for a week or two. Thereafter maintain a once or twice weekly watering.

SEEDTRAYS

Seeds sown in seedtrays need slightly different treatment as garden soil compacts in trays. Soilless growing mediums based on bark or peat give good results and, if well grown, the move from a soilless medium to soil should not have adverse effects.

Unless a soilless medium is nutrient enriched, however, seedlings will have to be fed soon after germination with a diluted liquid fertilizer or a hydroponic nutrient solution.

TRANSPLANTING

An advantage of transplanting is saving time. In late winter it is possible to start seeds under protection in seedtrays and plant out into the garden when the risk of frost is past. It shortens the period the crop occupies in garden space, so giving more latitude for bed preparation after the previous crop has been removed.

Hybrid cultivars are expensive and, if transplantable, financial savings can be made by small controlled sowings.

Gardeners should, where possible, grow their own transplants as the range of cultivars in seed packets is larger than that offered by vegetable plant nurseries.

In spring seedlings grown under protection should be hardened off for about a week to accustom them to the conditions under which they will grow. Ways of hardenings off are gradual reduction of water by less frequent watering, without allowing the soil to dry out, withholding fertilizer during that period, and removing all forms of protection.

In summer reduce shade cover gradually until there is no shade for at least a week prior to transplanting. Water reduction must be done with discretion and should not be reduced on cauliflowers.

Transplanting shock: Root loss can be as high as 50 per cent, causing an imbalance between the aerial parts of a plant and the roots. Usually the leaf area of a vegetable seedling is not reduced when transplanted but the root system is. This means that the foliage continues its normal rate of transpiration while the reduced root system is unable to take up sufficient moisture and nutrients to counter the loss and wilting occurs.

The amount of damage to plants grown in individual cell seedtrays will be considerably less than those grown in open containers or seedbeds. Recovery after transplanting is closely related to the extent of root damage.

With care, the result of transplanting shock can be over in a day or two. Longer checks may result in reduced yield and quality and a longer period to maturity. Transplants most likely to be adversely affected are bare-root ones taken from a seedbed, because there is a combination of root and soil loss. In summer these two losses can account for a high plant mortality. Reserve plants should be available.

In open containers or beds the closer the plants are together, the more root damage can be expected through intertwining.

It is preferable to transplant on a cool, overcast, windless day. Transpiration is high on hot, windy days.

Water is of prime importance. Before removing plants from trays or beds, water well. There are anti-transpirant products available which reduce plant transpiration for a period. Dipping plants in a solution of concentrate foliar feed also helps to reduce transplanting shock.

Seedlings should never be removed from trays or beds unless they can be planted immediately and should never be exposed to sun or wind for more than a few seconds. The older the plant, the greater the transplanting shock.

Soils which are to receive transplants should be in good condition and moist. The main requirement is water, but nutrients must also be available to be taken up by the damaged root system.

Dipping plants in a solution of concentrate foliar feed helps to reduce transplanting shock. Spraying plants in the seedbed with an anti-transpirant a short while before lifting also helps.

Commercial growers often use a starter solution based on various formulae using an application of 250 ml per plant. Starter solutions can aid rapid recovery from transplanting shock and can be a weak dilution of a proprietary liquid fertilizer high in nitrogen and phosphates, a hydroponic nutrient solution, a foliar feed composition, or any other product designed to get water and nutrients through the plant as quickly as possible.

After applying a starter solution or water, spread cutworm and snail bait around the plants and protect with a cutworm collar and shade-cap. Cutworm bait may also be raked into the top 10 to 20 mm of topsoil. If shade-caps are used, daily waterings are usually adequate; more frequent initial waterings may otherwise be needed. Shade-caps should be removed two to five days after transplanting, depending on weather conditions.

Once the plants are established, frequent light waterings should be reduced to twice weekly to encourage deeper rooting.

Poor seedlings: Discard weak and diseased seedlings. If growth is weak and spindly, the likely causes are too much shade, overcrowding, too much water or too high temperatures.

Stunted plants are usually the result of low soil fertility, yellow leaves indicate a lack of nitrogen, while purplish leaves may indicate a shortage of phosphates.

Tough, woody plants have been hardened off to an excessive degree. A poor root system may be caused by compaction or low soil fertility. Damping-off — a water-soaked, decayed stem near the soil line — is caused by overcrowding, poor drainage or aeration. If tackled in time, there are fungicides to control this disease.

6
Growing Systems

Commercial vegetable production has changed, developed and become more sophisticated, which has resulted in more efficient growing systems, higher yields, better quality produce, growing more in less space, and so on.

Much of the information gained from extensive worldwide research has been scaled down and adapted for vegetable gardeners, who may now apply these methods and improve their results through improved cultural techniques.

FLUID SOWING
England's National Vegetable Research Station developed the technique of fluid sowing pre-germinated seeds to reduce the 'hit or miss' chances of establishing plants from seeds at times when conventional sowing methods in seedtrays and seedbeds cause problems, such as in late winter or midsummer.

Seed germination can be started indoors under controlled conditions. Once the seeds have sprouted they are mixed in a jelly-suspension medium and sown in the beds.

A good example of how pre-germinated seeds can overcome unfavourable seedbed conditions for germination is lettuce seed. If near-surface soil temperatures are in excess of 30°C, seed becomes thermodormant and fails to germinate.

Germination of celery in seedtrays outdoors is difficult because, although seeds need light, the medium in which the seeds are placed can dry out. Pre-germinating seeds under controlled conditions does not pose a problem in establishing seedlings.

Pre-germinating slow-growing vegetables, such as parsley and parsnip, can give about two weeks' earlier emergence than normal sowing methods. Earlier growth is often linked with earlier harvesting and may also result in higher yields.

Careful sowing of pre-germinated seeds in a jelly suspension can also give more precision in spacing, which reduces the need for thinning and makes stands of plants more predictable.

All that is needed for fluid sowing is a plastic, lidded sandwich box lined with a layer or two of absorbent kitchen paper towel or similar material. The paper is thoroughly wetted and surplus water poured off. Seeds are sown thinly on the surface, not touching each other. The lid is replaced and the container kept at a temperature of 20 to 25°C.

Small-seeded vegetables should be kept at the lower temperature, while larger-seeded summer vegetables will germinate faster at 25°C. These are tomato, bush, lima and pole beans, cucurbits, eggplant and pepper. Light is essential for celery and witloof chicory and is preferred for lettuce.

The boxes should be checked daily as some seeds — lettuce, cucumber, kohlrabi, melon, radish, squash, sweet-corn and turnips — may germinate within one or two days under these conditions.

Roots of small-seeded vegetables should not be allowed to grow longer than 5 mm. Larger seeded ones may grow to about 10 mm before fluid sowing.

The seeds may not, however, germinate evenly. The decision when to sow will depend on when most of the seeds are at optimum root length. At this stage those with too-long roots or non-sprouted ones should be discarded.

If it is inconvenient to sow when the roots are at optimum length, root development can be arrested temporarily by placing the boxes in a refrigerator — *not* freezer — for up to 48 hours. If the refrigerator temperature is lower than 5°C, tomato, bean, eggplant, pepper, cucumber, melon and squash seedlings may be damaged or killed.

When ready to sow, the sprouted seeds should be washed carefully into a fine sieve and then tipped into a carrier jelly, such as cornflour made up with water or wallpaper paste. The jelly should be thick enough to hold the seeds in suspension. Avoid handling seeds and treat them carefully otherwise roots may be irreparably damaged.

The seed/jelly mixture should be placed in a clear plastic bag with one corner snipped off and can then be squeezed out along the pre-moistened row. The seeds should be covered in the normal way and watered if necessary. Some practice may be needed to sow evenly.

Pre-germinated seeds improve emergence, but well-prepared seedbeds are still necessary.

DEEP-BEDS

An alternative to the conventional 'open' vegetable garden is the deep-bed system. A deep-bed is an updated method of vegetable growing, previously referred to as the Chinese method or the Biodynamic-French intensive method.

High yields, space saving and the capacity for high-density planting are the main advantages of deep-beds.

Deep-bed cultivation gives considerable yield increases by reducing compaction to the minimum and making extra root area available to plants.

Deep-beds permit closer row and within-row spacings of a wide range of crops as additional soil depth and high fertility support extra root growth. Here, five lettuces are in a 1,5 m wide row.

A deep-bed is deeply cultivated by a type of double digging down to the full depth of a spade, then breaking up the subsoil to the full depth of a digging fork.

The first trench of topsoil is removed and taken to the far end of the bed where it is used as fill after the whole bed has been dug and forked. The second trench or row of topsoil is then placed on top of the broken-up subsoil of the first trench, the exposed subsoil of the second trench is broken up, and so it continues to the end of the bed.

In double digging, manure or compost is dug into the subsoil. Although it may also be done in deep-beds, the priority is to have a heavy application in the topsoil layer. This is done by spreading a thick layer on top of the beds before digging.

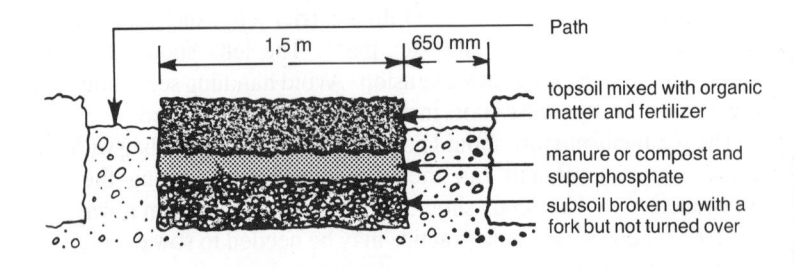

Cross-section of a deep-bed.

The emphasis on making sure the topsoil has a high content of organic matter is because the bed is slightly raised, there is no compaction and the soil has been cultivated to twice the normal depth, which would result in a rapid absorption of water down to the subsoil. A high organic-matter content helps retain moisture in the upper level.

Although deep-beds drain more freely than conventionally prepared beds — a disadvantage in Southern Africa — they compensate by retaining soil moisture through the high organic-matter content and roots are able to penetrate deeper to take advantage of moisture at lower levels.

Two important points: subsoil must never be brought to the surface; and once beds are prepared, they must not be walked on until crops are cleared and are again cultivated to ensure minimum compaction.

Deep-bed widths can vary between 1,2 and 1,5 m so that they can be worked on from paths on either side. Less than 1,2 m is wasteful because extra paths are then required, and more than 1,5 m makes it difficult to work in the centre of the bed. The length of a deep-bed should also be carefully considered: because it must not be walked on, a bed that is too long can be a nuisance.

Deep-beds must be completely level, particularly in summer when heavy rains can cause erosion on uneven or sloping soils.

After a deep-bed has been prepared, double digging should not be necessary again for two or three years. Each time a bed is cleared, heavy applications of organic matter should be dug into the topsoil to maintain a high humus level.

Vegetables may be sown or planted in blocks, bands or rows closer

Once deep-beds have been prepared they are not walked on. However, a plank across the bed will not compact the loose soil.

than conventional planting distances as the deep soil permits a more vertical root run.

Claims have been made that, because plants can be grown closer together in deep-beds, beds can produce up to four times the yield of a similar area under conventional growing methods. A more conservative estimate would be twice the yield.

SPACING

Recommendations for vegetable plant spacings in gardening books and other publications have not varied much over many years, and largely remain those originally determined by the types of implements used for commercial cultivation. These spacings were adapted for garden use, but experimental work in many countries has shown that much better use can be made of available space for vegetable beds.

Many of the conventional spacings are wasteful and unnecessary, often resulting in heading vegetables such as cabbage and lettuce being too large for the average family for one meal.

Closer spacing of a wide range of vegetables results in bigger yields of more convenient-sized crops. Distances between and within rows must always be balanced against the ultimate size of the crop.

Revised row and within-row spacings are given, where applicable, in the chapter on 'The Basic Vegetables', and do, in many instances, differ from standard recommendations.

It is important to realise, however, that closer spacings need a sufficiently high soil fertility to maintain the increased plant population.

Closer spacing may also involve some alteration in the layout of a vegetable garden. Long rows should be avoided. Rows running across 1,5 m wide beds are practical. Broad-band sowings are also useful for high fertility deep-beds.

Sowing and planting patterns have a bearing on close spacing and adaptions include square, diagonal, double-row and broad-band (wide row) planting.

Broad band: A band of closely spaced plants. An example is: In a bed 7 x 1 m three rows of bush beans, sown at 450 mm between rows and 150 mm between plants in the rows, would give about 140 plants. Using a broad-band the same area would have about 280 plants, which should mean twice the yield.

In broad-band sowing rows are planted across the bed instead of lengthwise with 150 mm between the rows and plants 75 mm apart. After germination plants in each row are thinned to 150 mm apart so they are then 150 mm square.

Good soil fertility and an increase of about 10 per cent of fertilizer will support a doubled-up plant population.

If staggered broad-band sowings are made in a bed, 300 mm should be left between each sowing to avoid older plants overshading young ones.

Broad-bands can be used for a number of vegetables, but early thinning is necessary to avoid overcrowding, which would result in poor yields through excessive competition or lack of light. Vegetables suitable for broad-band cultivation include: beet, carrot, kohlrabi, lettuce, onion, pea, radish, spinach, Swiss chard and turnip.

Double rows: Using double rows is another space saver, giving high yields for a number of vegetables. Optimum spacings are necessary to avoid overcrowding and cutting out of light. Vegetables suitable for double rows are: broad, bush and pole beans, beet, carrot, sweet-corn, single-stem tomatoes and turnip.

Square and diagonal: Where soil fertility is high, square and diagonal plantings can save space and at ideal spacings plants eventually come into contact with one another, providing shade for the soil and inhibiting weed growth.

Assuming that the soil fertility is uniformly adequate and plant spacings are right, the soil in the immediate vicinity of a plant's root

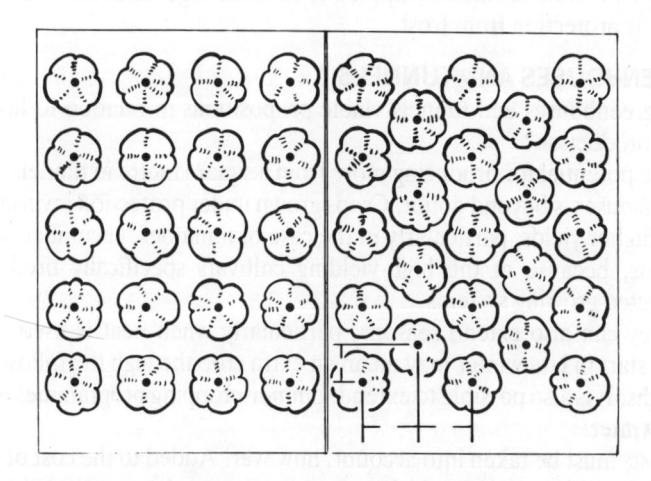

Beds are 1,5 m wide. The left bed, square planted at 400 mm, contains 20 plants. By diagonal planting with a 600 mm row spacing and 400 mm within-row, the plant population is increased to 23, with a similar amount of space between each plant.

system should provide sufficient nutrients and moisture without competition from neighbouring plants. That being the case, it may then be preferable to use diagonal planting: the plant population in a given area can be increased by reducing the row spacing while still giving each plant about the same amount of space above and below the soil level.

Vegetables suited to square and diagonal planting are: broccoli, Brussels sprouts, cabbage, cauliflower, self-blanching celery, leek, onion, parsley and Swiss chard.

HYDRO-GROWING

Hydro-growing is a simplified form of hydroponics — growing plants without soil — suitable for greenhouses, tunnels, patios receiving adequate sun, and other areas where container plants are grown.

One system uses specially formulated, porous, virtually indestructible clay pellets as an aggregate (inert growing medium) in 350 mm diameter and depth self-feeding plastic pots for large root system vegetables such as tomato, cucumber, melon, eggplant and pepper. Small, rectangular plastic containers standing in trough reservoirs are used for smaller vegetables and herbs.

Normally, pH testing for acidity or alkalinity is unnecessary as nutrient solutions are regularly topped up in the troughs and pots. Any of the available hydroponic solutions or powders may be used in the hydro-growing system.

This is an interesting and rewarding way of growing vegetables and it is often possible to extend cropping of summer vegetables into winter if there is protection from frost.

GREENHOUSES AND TUNNELS

Are greenhouses and tunnels viable propositions in relation to home food production?

The potential for producing more from a square metre in tunnels and greenhouses is beyond doubt. Crops grown under protection invariably give higher yields, particularly in the case of tomatoes, cucumbers and melons, because of the high-yielding cultivars specifically bred for protected growing systems.

They can also extend seasons, particularly when heat is used. An early start in late winter may mean an extra crop through the following months. It is also possible to extend summer-cropping programmes well into winter.

Costs must be taken into account, however. Added to the cost of the units, consideration should be given to the merits or otherwise of installing heating and the cost of using it. Other points to be considered are the replacing of tunnel plastic every few years, soil fumigation costs

A small, low, inexpensive, home-made tunnel can given an earlier start to plants in spring and extend cropping through into winter.

or, alternatively, using plastic planting bags or grow-bags.

In summer, tunnels and greenhouses are used to grow tomatoes, hothouse cucumbers, melons and possibly eggplants and peppers. In winter, in unheated units, most winter crops may be successfully grown, usually faster than outdoor ones, and strawberries can be forced into earlier cropping.

In order to merit the expense of a small tunnel or greenhouse, they would need to be in production throughout the year, but they can add yet another dimension to intensive vegetable gardening.

GROWING BY THE MOON

Gardening by the moon is a centuries-old practice. It is presumed it originated because man observed it worked, or seemed to work. It must also be presumed the idea endured because it had merit. It is known that the principles of moon gardening have been recognised over the centuries as fundamentally similar in many cultures which did not and could not have contact with each other. Growing by the moon was, therefore, a cultivation method independently discovered by many peoples.

The old saying that crops yielding their produce above ground should be planted on the waxing moon and those yielding below ground should be planted on a waning moon is an oversimplification and not entirely correct. Scientific studies have shown that planting on a waxing moon is advantageous to both above and below ground crops, while planting on a waning moon can be detrimental to most, with the exception of some root vegetables and one or two other crops.

Growing by the moon is not complicated. A calendar giving the moon phases and a current moon guide showing the moon signs — the 12 zodiacal signs — for each month plus an interpretation of the moon phases and signs are all that is needed.

Using moon phases alone may result in planting during an unfavourable sign within the period. Publications are available, adjusted to South African Standard Time, which give correctly calculated data.

When using this system it is important to use common sense and be flexible. There are specific times every month, depending on the season, that are suitable for sowing and planting. But it may not always be possible or convenient to follow the recommended dates, so alternatives should be used.

Moon phases: A calendar shows the moon phases as: new moon, first quarter, full moon and last quarter. They are sometimes translated as first, second, third and fourth quarters in moon-gardening publications and articles.

During the lunar month there is a period of increasing light — waxing — from new moon to full moon, and of decreasing light — waning — from full moon to new moon.

From new moon to the first quarter, mainly leaf vegetables are sown and planted — asparagus, broccoli, Brussels sprouts, cabbage, cauliflower, celery, endive, lettuce, parsley, spinach and Swiss chard. In addition there are pole beans, cucumber, garlic, kohlrabi and watermelon.

During the second phase of increasing light, from the first quarter to full moon, vegetables producing their yields above ground, mainly those producing fruits, are sown and planted — broad, bush, lima and pole beans, eggplant, melon, pea, pepper, pumpkin, squash, tomato and watermelon. Also included are chicory, garlic, leek, onion and Swiss chard. Some vegetables — pole bean, garlic, Swiss chard and watermelon — may be sown or planted in both periods.

There are in fact no hard and fast divisions. Vegetables in the first phase may be sown or planted in the second period and vice versa but, with the exception of chicory and leek, none should be sown or planted after full moon.

From full moon to the last quarter, decreasing light, root vegetables are sown — beet, carrot, chicory, leek, parsnip, potato, radish and turnip.

The last phase of decreasing light, from the last quarter to new moon is not a good time to sow or plant, but it may occasionally be necessary.

Moon signs: Each sign of the zodiac has an influence on sowing, planting and growth. The three water signs, Cancer, Scorpio and Pisces, are the most beneficial for plant growth while the moon is passing through them.

Taurus, Libra and Capricorn are fairly beneficial, while the remaining signs, Aries, Gemini, Leo, Virgo, Sagittarius and Aquarius are generally detrimental to plant life.

Aries: sowing and planting should be avoided on days when the moon is in Aries.
Taurus: a favourable sign for sowing and planting.
Gemini: an unfavourable sign.
Cancer: the most productive of all moon signs and used extensively for sowing and planting when the moon is passing through it.
Leo: an unfavourable sign.
Virgo: an unfavourable sign.
Libra: a favourable sign for several vegetables.
Scorpio: extensive sowings and plantings are made under this sign.
Sagittarius: an unfavourable sign, but can be used for sowing and planting onions if in the second period of increasing light.
Capricorn: a favourable sign for several vegetables.
Aquarius: an unfavourable sign.
Pisces: a very favourable sign for a wide range of vegetables.

Unfavourable signs should be avoided as far as possible for any sowing or planting unless there are exceptions such as for onions.

7
Successional Cropping

In most parts of Southern Africa vegetable gardens should be in production throughout the year. In some areas climatic conditions will preclude harvesting at certain times, but experimentation with different cultivars will often reduce the non-productive period to a minimum.

The aim should always be to have some fresh produce ready for harvesting every week of the year. At some stage most gardeners have 'feast or famine' periods, surpluses followed by periods when vegetables either have not reached maturity or have not been planted to provide continuous cropping.

Such periods can be influenced by climatic conditions but, more often, are the result of poor planning, which also leads to limited space for later successional sowings and plantings.

Careful planning will help to ensure regular cropping throughout the year.

The choice of cultivars also influences continuous cropping. For example, some cauliflowers are ready for harvesting seven to nine weeks from transplanting, late ones take 20 weeks or longer to produce heads, while others crop between these extremes. For most other vegetables more use must be made of successional sowings to spread the harvest period; there are few vegetables with cultivars of such a wide range of different maturity times.

Some cultivars perform better than others in a particular area, while in another area the reverse may apply. Finding the best cultivars for an area may mean growing several for a season or two, or getting local advice from gardeners or commercial growers.

Poor performances of cultivars because of poor adaptability can influence cropping succession. Fortunately, this occurs infrequently as improved cultivars reduce the risk. The range of high-quality cultivars available to vegetable gardeners is considerable.

Some cultivars have been specifically bred for growing at certain times of the year while others may have year-round adaption.

A careful choice of cabbage cultivars should be made to choose those best selected for the season. There are some lettuce cultivars suited to year-round production; others are recommended for specific seasons and usually give better results.

A parsley cultivar, bred for winter conditions, produces continuously during the cold months, through frost, but becomes coarse when grown in heat.

Some carrot cultivars perform better than others at certain times of the year in some areas. Testing two or three alongside each other in summer and winter for a couple of years will indicate which are best for a specific sowing time.

In summer, depending on the cultivar, carrots may be ready for harvesting between eight and 14 weeks from sowing, while in winter similar cultivars take from two to seven weeks longer to mature. All these are points which must be taken into consideration when planning succession sowing and harvesting.

Vegetables suitable for year-round production in many areas — beet, cabbage, carrot, leek, lettuce and Swiss chard — are important when planning continuity cropping.

Autumn and early winter sown root crops may usually be left in the soil after reaching maturity for several weeks without undue deterioration in cool weather, but continuity sowings of cabbage and lettuce must continue through winter, where possible, at about monthly intervals.

Vegetables with extended cropping periods may need sowing or planting only once or twice during the season to provide harvesting over several weeks or months. The important ones are: broad bean, broccoli, Brussels sprouts, kale and Swiss chard in winter, and pole and lima beans, cucumber, eggplant, New Zealand spinach, pepper, courgette squash, Swiss chard and tomato in summer.

Continuous cropping may be influenced by temperature variations such as poor or no germination in hot or cold soils, delayed germination, low temperatures restricting plant growth or hot temperatures influencing flower setting.

Within the optimum growing ranges, spring-sown vegetables double their growth rate with every 10 degrees rise in temperature, but when a plant reaches its maximum growth temperature it will be checked or stopped temporarily until temperatures fall back to the optimum growing range.

Water — usually the lack of it — can influence continuous cropping. Crops suffering from water stress invariably wilt or develop texture changes which result in delayed or reduced harvests. Those most likely to be affected first are the shallow-rooted kinds (see chapter on 'Watering').

Pests and diseases can disrupt a successional sowing and planting programme by reducing yields or even decimating entire sowings. Emerging seedlings and young transplants are particularly susceptible to attacks from various beetles, cutworms, grasshoppers, slugs, snails and damping-off.

Yield-reducing diseases include rust on beans, alternaria on carrots, powdery mildew on cucurbits and peas, and early and late blight on potatoes and tomatoes.

Keeping records will help with successful successional cropping and be invaluable when planning seasonal changes.

Example: Five bush-bean sowings in a bed.

Sown:	Harvest:	Cleared:
Sep. 15	Nov. 19	Dec. 10
Oct. 1	Dec. 3	Dec. 24
Oct. 22	Dec. 17	Jan. 7
Nov. 12	Jan. 3	Jan. 24
Nov. 26	Jan. 21	Feb. 11

Bed prepared for a three-sowing succession of carrots.

Sown:	Harvest:
Feb. 20	late May onwards
Mar. 12	late June onwards
Apr. 2	mid–late July onwards

Bed cleared and prepared for summer crops in August or early September.

Several points emerge from the example:
The five-spaced bean sowings should give continuous harvesting for about 12 weeks with an intended slight overlapping of harvesting to be safe.

When the final picking of beans has been made, the bed can be immediately prepared for a winter crop of carrots.

The first carrot sowing should be ready for harvesting in late May and, because soils are cold at harvesting time, lifting can be extended over a few weeks.

The harvesting period from the three sowings can extend over a 15-week period. Climatic limitations may necessitate adjustments in some areas.

Details of sowing times, approximate periods between sowing or planting and harvesting, and the estimated period of harvesting are given for all the vegetables in the chapter on 'The Basic Vegetables'.

INTERCROPPING

Intercropping is a way of ensuring the most use of available space in a bed as a temporary measure.

Fast-growing vegetables are intersown between slow-growing ones or those planted at wide spacings. They may also be grown in beds where later crops are planned.

Intercropping should never interfere with the main-crop vegetables, nor should intercropped vegetables be allowed to compete with the main crops for soil moisture and nutrients.

Vegetables suitable for intercropping are radish, looseleaf lettuce, lettuce (transplanted to save time), mustard spinach and spinach (cool weather only). Sweet-corn may be intercropped with wide-spreading vegetables such as trailing squash or pumpkins for a late harvest.

Intercropping should not be done between close-row plantings unless well in advance of the main crops, otherwise there will be overcrowding, detrimental to both intercrops and main crops.

Intercropping can be a useful extension to successional cropping if done sensibly.

See overleaf for a diagram showing intercropping in a long bed.

GROWING VEGETABLES

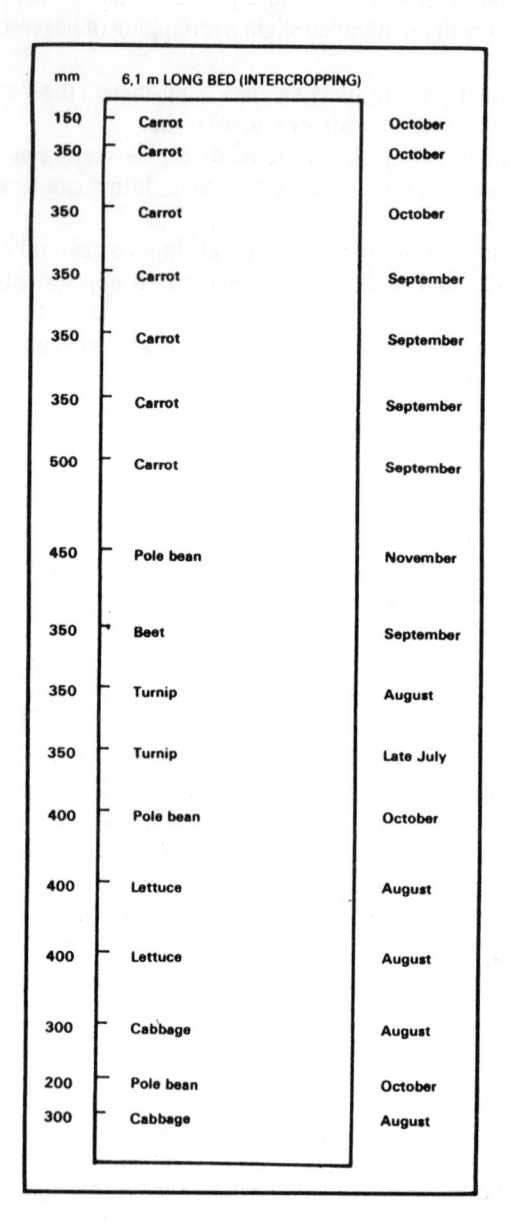

mm	6,1 m LONG BED (INTERCROPPING)	
150	Carrot	October
350	Carrot	October
350	Carrot	October
350	Carrot	September
350	Carrot	September
350	Carrot	September
500	Carrot	September
450	Pole bean	November
350	Beet	September
350	Turnip	August
350	Turnip	Late July
400	Pole bean	October
400	Lettuce	August
400	Lettuce	August
300	Cabbage	August
200	Pole bean	October
300	Cabbage	August

In this bed cabbage, lettuce, turnip and beet are intercropped between three rows of pole beans. Successional sowings of carrots are made over two months.

8
Container Growing

Container growing of vegetables is the answer for those who like and want to grow their own fresh produce but either have no garden, or a garden area that is too limited for vegetables.

People living in flats or townhouses and others who lack garden space can grow a wide range of vegetables if they have an open area with six or more hours of sun a day and space for a number of containers of different sizes and depths.

Growing vegetables in containers can be rewarding as well as productive, because the cost of growing them is often less than the conventional way. Less equipment is needed, they can be more efficiently supervised, there is little or no time-consuming weeding to be done, fertilizing and watering take less time and better pest and disease control can be achieved.

Many types of vegetables can be grown in containers. In some cases there are cultivars better suited to container growing than others. Vegetables with large root systems obviously need larger containers than those with less vigorous ones. Plants with indeterminate growth habits, such as pole beans, pole lima beans, most cucumbers, melons and some tomato cultivars, need support systems.

The main requirements for container vegetable gardening are: sufficient sun, enough space, adequate air circulation, good drainage, some way of disposing of surplus drainage water, and an accessible water supply.

Drainage is one of the most important points in successful container growing. Containers must have adequate drainage holes in their bases and the growing medium should also have good drainage properties, yet be adequately water retentive.

Saucers may be bought to fit small and medium plant pots and bases are often sold with asbestos-cement containers. Make sure the latter have drainage holes before planting.

Large containers without saucers or bases with drainage holes in the base should always be slightly raised above the floor or soil, leaving a sufficient gap for surplus water to drain away. It is important to avoid water accumulating in the growing medium at the bottom of the container and causing root rotting.

Consideration should also be given to providing large containers with some mobility, such as a set of rollers used for moving stoves, so they can be moved around as seasons change.

Containers: A number, specifically made for plants, are suitable if they are reasonably large and have a good depth.

Wooden wine barrels, cut in half horizontally, are sometimes available and make good growing containers. Metal drums, such as the 200-litre size often used for braais, cut lengthwise are ideal for shallow-rooting vegetables.

Wooden boxes can be used, but will have a limited life unless made of good hardwood or treated with a non-toxic preservative such as bitumen paint. Creosote, lead paints and other toxic materials should *never* be used. Boxes nailed or glued together are not as sturdy as ones with metal support bands.

Galvanised water baths are useful growing containers although they are not easy to disguise. Likewise, another ugly but effective plant container can be made of two, three or more old tyres stacked one on top of the other, supported on the inside to stop them overbalancing.

The larger sizes of black plastic nursery planting bags are suitable for a number of vegetables. The basal side drainage holes may need enlarging or increasing in number.

Plastic buckets and waste-paper baskets have limited use and concrete breeze-blocks with two cavities can be used for a few small-rooted herbs if they are not allowed to dry out.

Old metal or rubber dustbins may be used for growing potatoes, other large, deep-rooting vegetables and ones needing support with a solid base. They are also useful for long-rooted parsnips.

All containers have some advantages and disadvantages. Clay pots, wooden and asbestos-cement containers, to a degree, are porous, allowing excess moisture to evaporate through them. Following excessive watering it is an advantage, but in hot, dry conditions the growing medium may dry out rapidly.

Whatever container is used, it must have adequate drainage holes. If

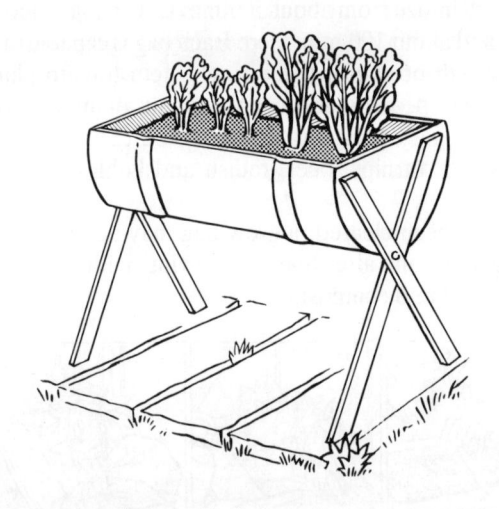

Metal drums, cut lengthwise, with drainage holes are ideal for a number of vegetables, mainly those with shallow root systems.

there is any risk of poor drainage, a 100 to 150 mm layer of pebbles, small stones or coarse gravel in the bottom should help.

Remember that plastic containers are not porous and the growing medium may remain too moist without good drainage. When new, they do not break easily, but after exposure to the sun for several months they may disintegrate.

Most vegetables need more or larger drainage holes then other container-grown plants as they are usually watered daily in the warm times of the year and, unless there is fast drainage, waterlogging in the lower parts of the container may occur.

Large, deep containers are, therefore, preferred for most vegetables for the best results. The minimum size is a diameter of 150 to 200 mm and a depth of at least 250 mm.

Select the containers best suited to the vegetables' growing needs, but also consider their appearance in the surrounding environment or landscape.

Grow-bags are used by commercial vegetable growers in tunnels and their value as containers for home-grown vegetables is considerable for those having limited space or diseased soils. A grow-bag is a sealed plastic bag containing a sterilised growing medium based on peat or bark. When placed in position, circular cuts are made in the top, the number depending on the vegetable to be grown, or most of the top is cut away for broadcast-sown seeds. The medium is thoroughly wetted, then about six drainage slits are made, about 100 mm long, in the base.

GROWING VEGETABLES

Grow-bags vary in size from about 500 mm to 1 m long, about 400 to 500 mm across and about 100 mm deep. Each bag is capable of supporting the root growth of two or three single-stem tomato plants, two cucumbers, melons, peppers and eggplants, six or more lettuces or small-headed cabbages and so on. Short-rooted carrots, such as Oxheart and Paris 108, turnips, beet, radish and kohlrabi may also be grown in them.

Once a crop has been cleared, a grow-bag may be used again for a non-related vegetable and after that the growing medium may be used as a mulch or turned into compost.

Grow-bags are ideal for cucumbers, melons, eggplants, peppers and tomatoes in tunnels and greenhouses, as well as a range of other vegetables under cover or outdoors.

Plants should never be allowed to dry out and will need regular feeding with a hydroponic mixture (centre).

Tall-growing plants should be supported in the same way as in the open garden (right).

Growing medium: Many gardeners make their own growing mediums because suitable ones are not always available at garden outlets.

A good medium is fast draining and water retentive so that it is evenly moist throughout the entire root zone area. A too-fast draining mix may cause water-stress problems, while a slow-draining one may cause root rotting. A commercial wetting agent or a few drops of liquid detergent (see 'Wetter Water' in the chapter on watering) will help to regulate optimum water capacity in most mixes.

There are basically two types of growing medium: one containing soil and the other soilless. Soil should not be used on its own in containers as it may compact or not hold sufficient moisture, depending on the texture.

A basic soil mix is equal parts by volume of garden soil, washed, sharp (gritty) river sand and peat, preferably imported. An alternative to peat is well-rotted manure or compost. If the manure or compost has been properly prepared, subjected to heat between 65 and 70°C, there should be no problems with soil pests, harmful bacteria, weeds or diseases.

Soil should preferably be sterilised before use, heated to 70 to 75°C in the oven or on the stove for about an hour, to kill off nematodes, harmful bacteria and fungi, soil pests, weeds and most virus diseases. Sterilised soil should not be used for at least two weeks as there may be a temporary build up of ammonium, manganese and sodium salts harmful to root systems.

The John Innes mix is seven parts soil, three parts peat and two parts sand, by volume, plus a John Innes (JI) base and lime. The base is two parts hoof and horn, two parts superphosphate and one part potassium sulphate, by mass. To each 18 litre (4 gallon) drum of JI mix add 10 g lime and 60 g JI base.

Soilless mixes are lightweight, fast draining, free of soil-borne diseases and easy to use and container handling is made easier than with those containing soil.

There are various soilless mix formulae: three parts peat (imported) and one part washed river sand, by volume. Another is six parts composted bark, one part peat and one part washed river sand, by volume. The sand may be replaced with vermiculite or perlite.

Variations of the peat/sand combination may be made from 100 per cent sand through to 100 per cent peat.

The JI base plus lime is suitable for soilless mixes. Soilless mixes contain few if any nutrients. Some commercially prepared mixes, however, are enriched with sufficient nutrients to feed plants for a few weeks. When growing vegetables in containers it should be assumed that feeding with a complete fertilizer formula will be necessary from soon after germination through to harvest, either in granular or liquid form. Liquid fertilizers are usually easier to handle and are less bulky.

Because container-grown vegetables need more frequent watering than those grown in the open garden, nutrients are leached from the mix more rapidly. Fertilizer applications should be adjusted by using at half strength twice as often to ensure that plants have access to readily available food at all times.

The frequency of fertilizing will depend on the type of vegetable, its stage of development, size of container and so on. Overfeeding can be as harmful as underfeeding.

Slow-release fertilizers, such as 5:1:5, are normally added to the mix once, when sowing or planting, as nitrogen is gradually released each time the mix is watered. Supplementary feeding, particularly with nitrogen, may be needed for long-term crops grown through summer because of daily watering.

Hydroponic powders, liquids and granular forms are suitable for soilless mixes.

GROWING VEGETABLES

It is often easier to start some vegetables such as brassicas, eggplant, leek, lettuce, pepper and tomato in seedtrays or small pots and then transplant into the final containers when large enough.

Watering is most important. Overwatering or underwatering are the main causes of disappointment when growing vegetables in containers. Late afternoon or evening hand watering is preferable, because the water penetrates overnight and is not rapidly evaporated by hot sun.

The mix in most containers dries out faster than most garden soils. Watering can, however, be reduced if containers are given a deep mulch. Mulching should be taken into account when filling containers so that space is allowed for up to 100 mm. Mulch can be added gradually as plants grow.

VEGETABLES SUITABLE FOR CONTAINER GROWING

Most vegetables may be grown in containers of the right size and depth. With some exceptions, the most suitable ones will grow in a confined area and produce an acceptable crop for the effort put into growing them, need little supporting, and have a determinate growth habit.

Artichoke, globe: Marginal, because of its extensive root system. A very large container is essential as it takes up a lot of space — up to a 2 m spread — is perennial and slow to produce flower heads.

Bean, broad: Marginal, as it may fail to set sufficient pods to compensate for the attention and space provided. Needs supporting.

Bean, bush: Suitable and may be individually grown in 200 mm diameter containers or spaced 150 mm square in larger containers. All cultivars are suitable.

Bean, lima: Bush cultivars, such as Fordhook 242, are suitable. They require a deeper container than bush beans and should be thinned to at least 300 to 400 mm apart otherwise they should be grown singly. Seed should be planted with the 'eye' downwards.

Bean, pole: Suitable, but needs 2 m supports on which to climb. All cultivars may be container grown.

Beet: Containers should be at least 200 to 300 mm deep. Space 75 to 100 mm between plants. Suitable cultivars are Detroit Dark Red, Cylindra and Formanova; the latter two, being cylindrical in shape, need a 300 mm depth.

Broccoli: Needs a large, deep container, preferably planted singly. F_1 hybrid cultivars are suitable. Green Sprouting Calabrese should not be grown.

Brussels sprouts: Need a large, deep container, one plant to a container. They should produce a good yield over several weeks. Use only F_1 hybrid cultivars. Some support may be needed in lightweight growing mixes.

Cabbage: Marginal, as they seldom warrant the time and effort needed to produce heads. Small-headed cultivars, such as Stonehead, are suitable for close planting, are fast growing, and can be grown in grow-bags.

Cabbage, Chinese: For autumn–winter production only. Plants need warmth for early development but cool conditions when approaching maturity otherwise they may bolt. A 200 to 300 mm diameter and depth container for individual plants is adequate, otherwise 150 to 250 mm between plants. Available cultivars are suitable.

Carrot: Containers should be 250 to 500 mm deep for standard cultivars. Shallower containers may be used for Oxheart and Paris 108. A lightweight mix is preferable. Thin to 75 to 100 mm each way.

Cauliflower: Not recommended. Any growth check may result in buttoning — small, inferior, immature heads.

Celeriac: Needs regular attention and plenty of water. Space 150 to 250 mm each way.

Celery: Marginal because of slow growth and high water requirements. If given careful attention and frequent waterings, container-grown plants could be more successfully grown than open-ground ones. Use Golden-Self-Blanching cultivar at 150 to 250 mm spacing each way.

Cucumber: Most tall-vined cultivars need large containers and support such as trellis or wires. Hothouse cucumbers are usually suitable for container growing. Pot Luck is a dwarf, bush cultivar suitable for growing in 200 mm diameter containers and hanging baskets. F_1 hybrid cultivars are preferred.

Eggplant: Needs a large, deep container or a grow-bag. Use high-yielding F_1 hybrids as single plants or two plants to a grow-bag.

GROWING VEGETABLES

Eggplants should be harvested with a sharp knife when half to almost fully grown. Skins should be bright and glossy.

Herbs: Most herbs are suitable for container growing. Container sizes vary with the type of plant growth.

Kale: Needs a large, deep container. The cultivar, Tall Green Curled, may need supporting in a lightweight mix.

Kohlrabi: A fast-growing vegetable. Allow 150 to 200 mm between plants. Use any available cultivar.

Leek: Requires a reasonably deep container, filled to about two-thirds. As the plants develop, add more growing medium to blanch stems. Close planting also assists blanching. Allow 100 to 150 mm between plants. All cultivars are suitable.

Lettuce: Ideal for container cultivation. Plants have shallow rooting systems and may be grown singly in small, 150 to 200 mm diameter containers or spaced 200 to 400 mm square, depending on the type grown. Leaf lettuce needs a 100 to 150 mm spacing each way as it is cut when immature and re-grown for a second cutting. Butterhead cultivars are spaced 200 to 300 mm square, while crispheads need the wider spacing. Check cultivars for seasonal suitability (see 'The Basic Vegetables').

Melon: Large, deep containers with strong supports for the vines are necessary. Most cultivars are suitable, F_1 hybrids usually produce higher yields.

Mustard spinach (greens): May be grown in small containers 50 to 75 mm apart each way in successional sowings.

New Zealand spinach: Needs plenty of space. Containers should be reasonably deep with a minimum diameter of 300 mm for a single plant or 500 mm for two plants. Regular leaf-tip harvesting is necessary for replacement growth. If protected, this summer spinach substitute may be overwintered.

Onion, salad: Most containers are suitable. Depth is not important so long as there is enough growing medium for the densely sown plants. Thin if necessary to 20 mm apart. White Lisbon and White Welsh are suitable cultivars.

Onion, multiplier: Grown from division of clusters, are also used as salad onions. Space about 200 mm apart each way.

Parsley: Requires a large, deep container. Allow about 200 mm between plants. Moss Curled is a summer cultivar, Decora is suitable for cooler months and overwintering.

Parsnip: Requires a large and very deep container. Space 75 to 100 mm apart.

Pea: A large, deep container is needed, support will be needed for all cultivars. Space 125 to 150 mm apart each way. Yields may be disappointing.

Pepper: Needs a large, deep container for single plants. Grow high-yielding F_1 hybrids for maximum yields.

Potato: A large, deep container, half barrel or similar, partially filled, planted and gradually topped up with growing medium to replace earthing up (hilling) in the open garden. Plant three or four tubers in a 500 to 600 mm diameter container.

Radish: Regular two to three weekly sowings in warm weather in small containers for continuity cropping. Sow thinly or thin to 20 mm apart. All summer cultivars are suitable.

Rhubarb: Marginal for containers. Needs a large deep container. If portable, the container may be placed in the dark in late winter to force new growth. It is a perennial and its value as a container plant depends on its yield potential. Yields may be increased if planted in soil with a high manure or compost content with a continuous high-fertility level when in active growth.

Squash, bush: Requires a large, deep container and plenty of space for plant spread, up to 1,5 to 2,0 m diameter. In containers 500 mm square two plants may be grown. Suitable cultivars include F_1 hybrid courgette types, F_1 hybrid Pans, summer squash, and Table King, winter squash, all with a bush growth habit.

Sweet-corn: Marginal, because of relatively low yield, plant size and the need for several plants to give cross-pollination. Allow up to 500 mm spacing each way and use F_1 hybrid cultivars.

Swiss chard: Needs a deep container, about 500 mm, for the vigorous root system. Minimum spacing between plants is 250 mm. All cultivars are suitable.

Tomato: Use large, deep containers or grow-bags and provide support, even for determinate (bush) cultivars. Plants should be grown singly in containers or two or three to a grow-bag. Planting distances depend on the type of tomato and whether pruned or unpruned (see Tomatoes in 'The Basic Vegetables').

Most cultivars may be container grown, but indeterminate ones, those that continue making new growth unlike self-stopping, determinate ones, need strong supports.

Determinate cultivars include: Bonus VFN, Flora-Dade, Floramerica and Heinz 1370.

An indeterminate one bred for home-garden use is Early Cascade. Small-fruited cultivars include: Toy Boy and Small Fry.

Most cultivars can be adapted to container growing.

Turnip: A fast-growing vegetable suitable for containers and grow-bags. Thin to 50 mm between plants and harvest when golf-ball size. Snowball is earlier than most other available cultivars.

Watercress: Must have continuous, very moist growing conditions and prefers some shade in summer. Plant spacing is 200 mm each way. More adaptable to cool conditions than summer when pests are a problem.

Above: A section of the author's vegetable garden: in the foreground, onions approaching maturity; at the back, a part-bed of broad beans with bags of compost ready for digging into the deep-beds. New transplants have shade-cap covers.

Below: Summer mulching reduces the need for watering.

Globe artichokes are a delicacy, but are slow growing and need plenty of space.

A high production deep-bed.

Broad beans need cool growing conditions throughout their growing span.

Regular picking of bush beans encourages new flower and pod formation.

Above: Pre-germinated seeds in suspension ready for fluid sowing.

Pods of lima beans should be well filled and bulging when harvested.

The crown (main) head of broccoli, ready for cutting.

Below: Brussels sprouts perform best under cool to cold growing conditions.

Round-headed cabbage cultivars are harvested when hard.

High density-sown carrots at 150 mm row spacings.

Below: A well-grown cauliflower should have a compact, heavy, smooth white head.

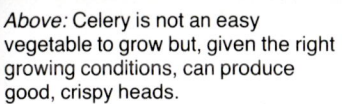

Above: Celery is not an easy vegetable to grow but, given the right growing conditions, can produce good, crispy heads.

Above right: Chicory is grown for winter forcing of 'chicons'.

Right and below: An early crop of tunnel-grown cucumbers.

Above: Kale (borecole) can be used as a cabbage or spinach substitute and has a long cropping period.

Above left: Well-grown eggplants will produce fruits over a long period through summer and autumn.

Left: Intercropping fast-growing lettuce with long-term leeks.

Right: Deep-bed-grown parsnips.

Below: Leeks are ridged to encourage longer, blanched stems.

Above: When onion tops topple they are ready for harvesting and drying.

Left: Tunnel-grown melons.

Above and below: Peppers produce high yields over a long period if they receive no early growth check.

Left: Best potato yields are obtained from early spring planting.

Radishes are fast growing, easy to grow and should be harvested while young.

Swiss chard growing in a small hydro-growing container.

Above: No summer vegetable garden is complete without tomatoes.

Above left: Small Fry, F_1 hybrid tomato, is small fruited but earlier than most other cultivars.

Below: Hydro-grown turnips.

Below: Tomatoes in a grow-bag. The hole in the centre facilitates feeding and watering.

9
Harvesting

The greatest sense of achievement in growing vegetables is to harvest them, see them displayed on the dining-room table and then enjoy their excellent flavour. But to ensure that this pleasure is not in any way reduced, it is important to pay particular attention to how and when the crops are harvested. It would be a pity to lose some of the advantages of good growing techniques through incorrect harvesting.

Harvesting vegetables is often delayed too long in order to get more — be it from numbers, size or mass — often resulting in less because of more wastage and a reduction in quality.

The approach to harvesting should be a balanced one, where crops are harvested when young, but refrain from taking them at a too-young stage when final yields may suffer.

Seasonal variations also influence harvesting. In cooler months crops often yield over longer periods and do not deteriorate rapidly after reaching maturity as they do in summer. In hot weather more frequent harvesting is necessary to maintain quality.

Precooling is the rapid removal of 'field heat' from freshly harvested produce to slow the process of ripening and reduce deterioration. Vegetables picked in the cool of early morning or in late evening when field heat is lower than during the day, will usually keep better than those harvested in hot conditions unless immediately precooled.

Deterioration of freshly harvested produce depends on a number of factors: respiration rate, temperature, moisture content, physical damage and the particular crop's resistance to water loss. Precooling reduces respiration rate, slows deterioration and often retards any decay present. Ideally, produce should be brought down to a temperature between 0 and 5°C as quickly as possible.

The respiration rate is the key to maintaining the highest degree of quality in post-harvest vegetables. Crops with low respiration rates, such as onions and potatoes, usually have the longest storage life. Then follow beet, Brussels sprouts, cabbage, carrot, celery, cucumber, melon, pepper, squash, tomato and turnip.

Poor-keeping, high respiration rate vegetables are: asparagus, beans, broccoli, cauliflower, lettuce, New Zealand spinach, peas, sweet-corn and Swiss chard.

Careful handling when harvesting and storing also helps in maintaining high quality.

WHEN TO HARVEST

Artichoke, globe: Immature flower buds should be cut when they are 50 to 100 mm in diameter, leaving 50 mm of stem attached. If the bud begins to open before cutting, quality deteriorates. Jerusalem artichokes are grown for their tubers and may be lifted any time after foliage dies back through winter, but before regrowth starts in spring.

Asparagus: 'White' asparagus is cut with a sharp knife just as the tips break the soil surface, leaving about 150 mm of stem. Green asparagus is allowed to grow above ground up to a height of 200 mm when it is cut, but earlier if tips begin to open. Stalks should be tender for almost their full length.

Bean, broad: Pods may be used when young but this is wasteful. Pods should swell and be harvested while the seeds are plump and the scar on the shelled bean is white, cream or green. A black scar indicates over-maturity.

Bean, bush and pole: Pods should be well filled and bright coloured, snap easily and show little or no signs of fibre. A few cultivars have 'strings' and will snap only when very young. Thick, tough pods are overmature.

Bean, lima: Pods should be well filled and bulging. After shelling, size grading may be advisable as there may be a difference in cooking time between almost mature and slightly younger beans.

Beet: Roots should be smooth and without scales around the top. Cylindrical cultivars grow partially out of the soil. Globe cultivars should be harvested at golf-ball size, while cylindrical ones should have a diameter of about 40 mm.

Broccoli: Plants produce a main crown (head) similar to a cauliflower, which should be cut off when fully developed, but before the compact flower buds start to open, with 100 to 150 mm of stem. Numerous smaller side shoots develop after the crown has been harvested. Although smaller, they are harvested in a similar manner.

Brussels sprouts: Plants produce sprouts from the base upwards. Usually the bottom sprouts are blown — loose — and should be discarded. As sprouts develop and become firm, they should be picked. If left on the plant too long, they split and deteriorate. Gradual stripping of leaves encourages quicker sprout development. When half to two-thirds of the plant has been harvested the open head at the top may be removed to encourage the top sprouts to form, and used as a small cabbage.

As Brussels sprouts develop, sprouts form from the base upwards and should be picked as soon as they become firm. Gradual leaf stripping encourages faster sprout development.

Cabbage: Round-headed cultivars should be hard when harvested, conical ones are usually softer but often have a better texture and flavour. If too many heads mature at the same time, pull plants upwards slightly to disturb the root system, which slows down water intake and delays splitting of the heads.

They may be harvested any time after reasonably solid heads form. Although some cultivars do not split as quickly as others, quality still declines after reaching full maturity.

Cabbage, Chinese: When the head is well formed, compact and fairly solid it is ready for harvesting. Outer leaves should be removed as they may be tough and bitter.

Carrot: The optimum stage for harvest is when roots are about 25 mm in diameter, although they may grow thicker in cool weather. Too-large roots are often tough and lacking in flavour. Continuity sowings should ensure a plentiful supply of young carrots.

Cauliflower: Heads should be compact, white and smooth. Exposure to sun accelerates coarseness and causes discoloration. As heads develop, they should be covered by breaking leaves over them or tying the leaves together. Mature heads vary in size according to the cultivar. 'Riceyness' of heads — individual flower stalks pushing upwards — may indicate overmaturity, poor growing conditions, an unsuitable cultivar for the area, lack of water or too high temperatures.

Celery: Self-blanching cultivars should be 300 to 400 mm tall from leaf tips to base. Outer leaves should be discarded, inner ones should be white. Crispness is largely dependent on growing conditions. Cool weather improves quality.

Celeriac: Thickened stem-root 'bulbs' should be harvested when 70 to 100 mm in diameter. Flesh should be firm and crisp; overmature celeriac is fibrous.

Chicory: Forced, blanched immature heads should be cigar-shaped with tightly folded leaves of creamy white. If light penetrates, heads unfold and leaves become discoloured. A slight bitterness is a feature of forced chicory.

Cucumber: Fruits should be bright green and not fully mature. Overmature fruits are large, have a dull skin, an enlarged seed cavity and tough seeds. Hothouse cucumbers with swollen sections or shrivelled ends are usually bitter. Almost mature fruit size varies according to the cultivar.

Cucumbers grown for cocktail pickles are harvested at about 50 mm while dill-pickle cucumbers are harvested at about 100 mm.

Eggplant: Fruits are cut from the plant with a sharp knife when half grown up to almost full size. Through these stages they should be firm, heavy, smooth with a shiny skin, uniformly purple.

Overmature fruits have dull skins, possibly discoloured, and are likely to be soft or shrivelled with inferior flesh and bitter seeds.

Garlic: Harvest when tops die down and the skin of the bulbs, made up of a number of cloves or segments, have a papery texture.

Kale: Pick outer leaves while young, fresh and tender. Overmature leaves turn yellow-green. Frequent picking of outer leaves encourages new leaf growth.

Kohlrabi: Roots — thickened stems — are harvested after they reach a diameter of 50 mm up to 100 mm. Old roots become tough and fibrous. Quality is better if plants make rapid growth.

Leek: May be harvested as soon as they are big enough to eat. Quality and length will be improved if stems are blanched by hilling soil against them. Stem thickness can vary between 20 and 50 mm. Overwintered leeks may be tough, but if sliced thinly this is not a problem.

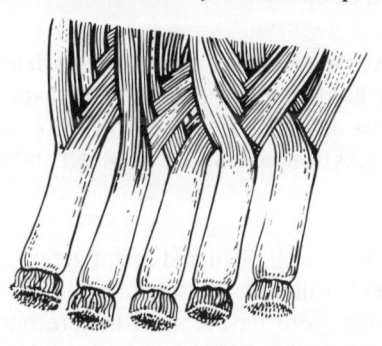

The quality and length of leeks will be improved if stems are blanched by hilling soil against them.

Lettuce: Heading lettuce — crisphead and butterhead — should have firm heads when harvested. Firmness should be tested with the back of the hand, not by pinching. Leaf lettuces do not produce firm heads and are grown for their young leaves. Lettuce may become bitter in hot weather. Hard, pale yellow heads indicate overmaturity.

Melon: A ripe melon is usually detectable by the typical melon aroma at the flower (base) end of the fruit. It should feel heavy and the fruit may separate from the stem; also a complete circle of a fine crack may appear at the base of the fruit.

New Zealand spinach: As soon as plants are large enough tip stems are cut off. Frequent harvesting encourages new growth.

Okra: Pods must be immature, up to 120 mm long and bright green. Overmature pods lose colour and become hard, stiff and inedible.

Onion: When tops turn yellow and topple, bulbs are ready for harvesting, curing, drying and storing. Thick-necked and bolting onions should be used quickly as they do not store. Long-day cultivars have a longer storage life than short-day ones.

Onion, salad: Green onions may be harvested as soon as they are large enough. As they increase in size, so they become more pungent.

Parsley: Outer leaves should be picked when large enough to encourage new growth from the centre of the plant. Regular picking is necessary otherwise replacement leaves are slow forming. Old, tough leaves lack the bright-green colour.

Parsnip: Uncover the shoulder of the root to determine the potential root size: from 40 to 70 mm should provide mature roots. An idea of maturity may also be gained from the growing period by checking roots after 20 to 25 weeks from sowing during winter and about 20 weeks from a spring sowing.

Pea: Pods should be well filled and bright green. A check by opening two or three pods will indicate maturity. Slightly immature peas are sweeter and have more flavour than mature ones. Overmaturity is indicated by yellow and wrinkled pods and wrinkled, pale peas.

Pepper: Peppers may be harvested from half size to full size. In early stages, depending on the cultivar, fruits are a glossy medium to dark green or bright yellow with firm flesh. After reaching full size they ripen and usually turn red. Green peppers are more popular. Overmature fruits have wrinkled, soft skins.

Potato: May be harvested as soon as the tubers are large enough, from egg size upwards. While plants are in active growth tubers will continue to increase in size. Young tubers do not keep long. See also Potatoes under 'The Basic Vegetables'.

Pumpkin: Fruits are usually allowed to remain on vines until plants are dead, then they are fully ripe. Skins should be firm, glossy and impervious to scratching.

Radish: Radishes are harvested before they reach full size, from 20 mm in diameter upwards. They should be plump, firm without interior pithiness.

Radish is the easiest of all vegetables to grow. Under good growing conditions roots can be harvested 20–30 days from sowing.

Rhubarb: Young, two-year old plants should not be harvested for more than two or three weeks in a year. Not more than two-thirds of leaf stalks should be picked at any one time from older plants. Stalks should be pulled off and not cut. Rhubarb leaves contain soluble oxalic acid and are highly poisonous.

Shallot: Harvest when tops die down, lift and remove dead foliage when completely dry. Clumps may be left intact until required.

Squash: Courgette squash — baby marrows — are harvested at a very immature stage, when 75 to 150 mm long, three to four days after the flower opens.

Summer squash, depending on the type, are harvested at an immature stage through to almost fully grown. Skins should be sufficiently soft to be broken by a thumbnail. They have a short storage life.

Winter squash should be allowed to ripen on the vines unless heavy frosts are expected. Fruits should always be harvested with a short piece of stem attached. A well-cured winter squash has a tough skin, is impervious to scratching, and is without blemishes, cuts or abrasions. The storage period depends on the cultivars grown.

Sweet-corn: Cobs should be harvested when almost fully grown with kernels at the 'milk' stage. Kernels are then almost full size, soft, tender and filled with an opaque milky juice. Avoid opening the husks to check on kernel size as pests and birds may then cause damage.

At the milk stage the silks at the tips of the cobs are brown and dry. When the silks first appear cobs are well formed and, depending on the weather, it takes 15 to 25 days for the silks to dry — an indication that cobs are ready for picking.

Sweet-corn is at its best when kernels are almost full size. They are then at the 'milk' stage and the silks, at the top of the cob, are brown and dry.

Swiss chard: Plants should be well established before cutting, about seven to nine weeks from germination. Outer leaves are cut about 25 mm above ground. As outer leaves are removed, new ones form from the central growing point. Regular cutting encourages vigorous leaf development.

Tomato: Fruits should be vine-ripened for best flavour, colour and sugar content. If they have to be picked when changing colour from green, they will ripen best at temperatures between 15 and 22°C. Ripening picked tomatoes in full sun may reduce quality.

Turnip: Roots are harvested when 50 to 75 mm in diameter. In hot weather they may become pithy with a bitter flavour, even before reaching edible size.

Watermelon: Ripeness is not easy to determine, although rapping fruits sharply with knuckles can remove some guesswork. A crisp, metallic sound indicates immaturity, but if it is a dull, flat sound the fruit is probably ready for harvesting. Another indication is that where the fruit lies on the soil, the skin colour changes from white to light yellow.

STORING FRESHLY HARVESTED VEGETABLES

Ideally, vegetables should be eaten when they are fresh as they deteriorate from the time they are harvested at varying rates.

The life of harvested vegetables can be extended by providing them with optimum temperatures and relative humidity. In domestic refrigerators it is not possible to provide such conditions, because vegetables have varying temperature and relative humidity requirements.

The following is a guide to the time fresh vegetables should be stored in a domestic refrigerator without undue deterioration:

Vegetable	Time	Notes
Artichoke, globe	5 to 7 days	
Asparagus	2 to 7 days	Trim bases and stand in ice or shallow water.
Bean, broad	3 to 5 days	
Bean, bush and pole	3 to 7 days	
Bean, lima	3 to 5 days	
Beet	7 to 14 days	Moisten roots.
Broccoli	3 to 7 days	
Brussels sprouts	3 to 7 days	
Cabbage	7 to 14 days	
Cabbage, Chinese	5 to 10 days	Remove outer leaves.
Carrot	7 to 20 days	Moisten roots, remove tops.
Cauliflower	5 to 10 days	
Celery — celeriac	7 to 14 days	
Chicory, forced	3 to 7 days	
Cucumber	3 to 7 days	
Eggplant	3 to 7 days	Avoid bruising.
Kale	3 to 7 days	
Kohlrabi	7 to 14 days	Moisten roots.
Leek	7 to 14 days	Remove old leaves.
Lettuce	3 to 5 days	Avoid too much moisture.
Melon	3 to 7 days	Avoid bruising.
New Zealand spinach	3 to 5 days	Keep well ventilated.
Okra	3 to 5 days	
Onion, salad	1 to 4 days	Keep well ventilated.
Parsley	3 to 5 days	Keep well ventilated.

Parsnip	7 to 14 days	Moisten roots.
Pea	1 to 3 days	Keep well ventilated.
Pepper	3 to 7 days	Avoid bruising.
Pumpkin	variable	Keep cut parts covered.
Radish	7 to 14 days	Keep well ventilated.
Rhubarb	7 to 14 days	Trim bases and stand in shallow water.
Squash, courgette	3 to 7 days	
Squash, summer	7 to 14 days	Keep cut parts covered.
Squash, winter	variable	Keep cut parts covered.
Sweet-corn	1 to 3 days	Coldness helps retain sugar.
Swiss chard	3 to 5 days	Keep well ventilated.
Tomato	7 to 10 days	Avoid bruising.
Turnip	7 to 14 days	Moisten roots.
Watermelon	7 to 10 days	Keep cut parts covered.

Garlic, onion, potato, shallot, squash and pumpkin (uncut) have variable storage periods in non-refrigerated storage facilities.

10
The Basic Vegetables

Complete success in growing vegetables can never be guaranteed because there are many factors influencing growth over which the gardener has little or no control. The risks of failures or poor yields can, however, be reduced through a knowledge of the requirements of each vegetable. In previous chapters various facets of vegetable growing have been discussed and, when linked with the basic information in this chapter, many problems can be overcome or avoided.

In many respects vegetable gardening is more complex than commercial vegetable growing. For example, many gardeners have beds containing several different types of vegetables, probably with differing specific requirements. For this reason, there must be a compromise to try and get the best out of each.

BASIC FERTILIZER PROGRAMME
This is a general guide for vegetable gardeners who do not have soils tested on a regular basis. In beds of mixed vegetables a compromise is necessary, but because it is a basic programme adaption is simple.

200g/m^2 superphosphate dug into the bed in late winter or spring.

100g/m^2 2:3:2(22) or 2:3:4(24) dug in just before sowing and planting in spring and repeated for the winter programme.

Supplementary nitrogen as a side-dressing in a band 50 to 100 mm away from plants beside the rows with LAN (limestone ammonium nitrate) in single or split applications for specific crops.

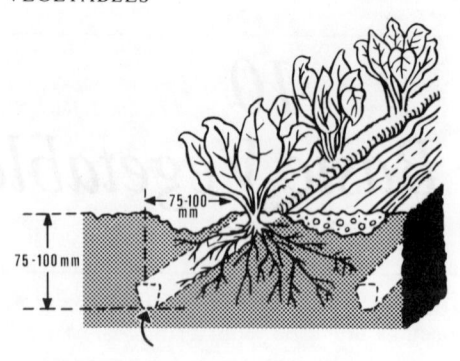

Supplementary nitrogen side-dressings are given to most crops during growth as a band 50-100 mm away from the plants. The fertilizer is then well watered in where it will become available to the plants' roots.

LAN application as a side-dressing for each 1 m row*:
25g (single application): beet, broad beans, carrot, parsnip, turnip and winter radish.
50 g (split into two applications): bush, lima and pole beans, broccoli, cucumber, eggplant, garlic, leek, lettuce, melon, onion, pepper, pumpkin, squash, sweet-corn, tomato, watermelon.
100 g (split into two applications): Brussels sprouts, cabbage, cauliflower, celery, kale, New Zealand spinach, potato, parsley, Swiss chard.

Avoid placing LAN on foliage or any part of plants, water in well.

*One level matchbox is about 20 g LAN.

SOWING DEPTHS

Every effort should be made to sow seeds at the correct depth as it may influence germination and ultimate yields. Sowing depth is a critical factor in the germination of a few vegetables marked*.

Where soils are known to crust, care should be taken to maintain constant moisture from seed sowing to germination. The same applies to shallow-sown seeds.

A guide to sowing depths:

5 to 10 mm	Celery*, celeriac*, chicory*, eggplant*, lettuce*, parsley*, pepper*.
10 to 20 mm	Beet*, broccoli, Brussels sprouts, cabbage, carrot, cauliflower, chives, endive, kale, kohlrabi, leek, okra, onion, parsnip, radish, spinach, tomato, turnip, swede.

20 to 30 mm   Artichoke (globe), asparagus, cucumber, melon, squash, Swiss chard, watermelon.
30 to 40 mm   Bean (bush, lima, pole), New Zealand spinach, pumpkin.
40 to 50 mm   Bean (broad), pea, sweet-corn.

SPACING GUIDE

For most of the basic vegetables a guide to conventional row and within-row spacings is given, together with spacings for high-density growing. If high-density spacings are used, soil fertility must be high. Strict disease and pest control is also important. They are recommended for deep-beds, but should be adjusted if necessary.

CULTIVARS

Listed cultivars are available in various-sized packets. They have all been grown in South Africa under a wide range of conditions. This is a condensed list and does not imply that unlisted cultivars are necessarily inferior.

Bean, broad	Aquadulce	
	(Aquadulce longpod)	
Bean, bush	Harvester	
	Rolito	
	Seminole	
	Topcrop	
	Winter Green	
Bean, lima	Fordhook 242	Bush
	Large Speckled Pole	Pole
Bean, pole	Blue Peter	
	Lazy Housewife	
	Witsa	
Beet	Crimson Globe	
	Cylindra	Cylindrical roots
	Detroit Dark Red	Globe
	Detroit Dark Red Short Top	Globe
	Formanova	Cylindrical roots
Broccoli	Dandy Early	F_1 hybrid
	Green Duke	F_1 hybrid
	Premium Crop	F_1 hybrid
Brussels sprouts	Captain Marvel	F_1 hybrid
	Jade Cross E	F_1 hybrid

GROWING VEGETABLES

Cabbage	Big Cropper	F_1 hybrid
	Cape Spitz	Mainly winter
	Cape Spitz Summer	Mainly summer
	Gloria	F_1 hybrid, year-round
	Grand Slam	F_1 hybrid, mainly autumn
	Hercules	F_1 hybrid, year-round
	NS Cross	F_1 hybrid, year-round
	Red Rock	
	Spitzo	F_1 hybrid, mainly winter, Cape Spitz type
	Stonehead	F_1 hybrid, mainly spring and autumn, small heads
Cabbage Chinese		Try some of the newer hybrids which are slower to bolt
Carrot	Cape Market	
	Chantenay Karoo	
	Chantenay Red Core	
	Chantenay Royal	
	Gold King	
	Ideal Red	
	Kuroda	
	Nantes	
	Oxheart	
	Paris 108	Round – for containers
	Scarlet Nantes	
	Tarenco	F_1 hybrid
Cauliflower	Canberra	Late
	Rami	F_1 hybrid, very early
	Snowball Y	
	Snowcap	Late, large heads
Cucumber (outdoor)	Ashley	
	Cherokee 7	Pickling
	National Pickling	
	Pot Luck	Dwarf – for containers
	Special Rust Resistant	
	Stono	
	Sweet Slice	
	Triumph	F_1 hybrid
	Victory	F_1 hybrid
Cucumber (hothouse)	Pepinova	F_1 hybrid
	Pepinex	F_1 hybrid
	Teto	F_1 hybrid, also outdoors
Eggplant	Black Beauty	
	Florida High Bush	
	Midnite	F_1 hybrid
Leek	Broad Flag	
	Carentan	
	Italian Giant	

THE BASIC VEGETABLES

Lettuce	*March-June sowing for winter production*	
	Butterhead cultivars	
	Climax 84	Crisphead
	Grand Rapids	Looseleaf
	Great Lakes 659	Crisphead
	Paris White Cos	Cos
	Queen Crown	Crisphead
	Wintercrisp	Crisphead
	July-September sowing for spring harvesting	
	Citation	Butterhead
	Commander	Crisphead
	Great Lakes 659	Crisphead
	Kagraner Sommer	Butterhead
	Grand Rapids	Looseleaf
	October-December sowing for summer cropping	
	Great Lakes 659	Crisphead
	Grand Rapids	Looseleaf
	Robinvale	Crisphead
	King Crown	Crisphead
	January-March sowing for autumn harvesting	
	Citation	Butterhead
	Commander	Crisphead
	Grand Rapids	Looseleaf
	Great Lakes 659	Crisphead
	Kagraner Sommer	Butterhead
Melon	Imperial 45	
	Ogen PMR	
	Saticoy	F_1 hybrid
Onion	Bon Accord	
(short-day)	Granex 33	F_1 hybrid
	Pyramid	
	Texas Grano	
(long day)	Australian Brown	
	Caledon Globe	
(salad)	White Lisbon, White Welsh	
Parsley	Decora	Winter only
	Moss Curled	
Parsnip	Guernsey	
	Hollow Crown	
Pea	Greenfeast	
	Kelvedon Wonder	
	Sugar Snap	

GROWING VEGETABLES

Pepper	Bell Boy	F_1 hybrid, sweet
	California Wonder	Sweet
	Komati	Sweet
	Long Red Cayenne	Hot
	Serrano	Hot
Pumpkin	Ceylon's	
	Flat White Boer A	
	Flat White Boer Van Niekerk	
	Queensland Blue	
Radish	Black Spanish	Winter
	Cherry Belle	
	French Breakfast	
	Sparkler	
	White Icicle	Long
Squash	Ambassador	F_1 hybrid, bush, courgette
	Blackjack	F_1 hybrid, bush, courgette
	Early Butternut	F_1 hybrid, trailing, winter squash
	Gold Rush	F_1 hybrid, bush, courgette
	Golden Hubbard	Trailing, winter squash
	Green Hubbard	Trailing, winter squash
	Longzini	F_1 hybrid, bush, courgette
	Patty Pan	F_1 hybrid, bush, summer squash
	Rolet	Trailing, improved Little Gem
	Sunburst	Patty pan type
	Spaghetti	
	Table King	Bush, winter squash
	Table Queen	Trailing, winter squash
	Waltham	Trailing, winter squash
Sweet-corn	Commander	F_1 hybrid
	Jubilee	F_1 hybrid
Swiss chard	Fordhook Giant	
	Lucullus	
Tomato	Bite Size	Cocktail type
	Diego	F_1 hybrid
	Flora-Dade	
	Heinz 1370	
	Karino	
	Oxheart	
	Piersol	
	Roma VF	
	Rossol	

Turnip	Early Purple Top Globe
	Snowball
Watermelon	Black Diamond
	Charleston Gray
	Congo
	Sugar Baby

YIELDS

At conventional within-row spacings, the following yields may be expected from a 1 m row unless otherwise stated. Yields from high-density rows and deep-beds should be higher in most cases.

Bean, broad (shelled)	1,0 to 2,0 kg
Bean, bush	2,0 to 2,5 kg
Bean, lima (shelled)	800 g to 1,0 kg
Bean, pole	2,5 to 3,5 kg
Beet	1,5 to 2,5 kg
Broccoli	1,5 to 2,0 kg
Brussels sprouts	1,5 to 2,5 kg
Cabbage	2 to 3 heads
Carrot	1,0 to 2,0 kg
Cauliflower	1,5 to 2,0 kg
Cucumber (outdoor)	20-plus fruits a plant
Cucumber (tunnel)	20-plus fruits a plant
Eggplant	20-plus fruits a plant
Leek	5 to 15 stems
Lettuce	3 to 6 heads
Melon (outdoor)	5-plus fruits a plant
Melon (tunnel)	10-plus fruits a plant
New Zealand spinach	2,0 kg plus
Onion, bulb	1,5 kg plus
Parsley	300 to 500 g
Parsnip	2,0 kg plus
Pea (pods)	1,0 kg plus
Pepper	20-plus fruits a plant
Potato	2,5 kg plus
Radish	500 to 700 g
Squash — courgette	30 to 50 fruits a plant
Squash — summer	1,5 kg plus a plant

GROWING VEGETABLES

Squash — winter	3,0 kg plus a plant
Sweet-corn	2 to 3 cobs a plant
Swiss chard	1,5 kg plus
Tomato	2,5 kg plus a plant
Turnip	1,0 to 2,0 kg
Watermelon	2 to 6 fruits a plant

DIAGONAL PLANTING

Where space is at a premium, transplantable vegetable populations can be increased by diagonal planting. Row spacing is increased, within-row spacing is kept at the same distance, but plants are offset, thus giving a similar distance between plants, as in square spacing. The illustration below shows how to increase a plant population within a given area.

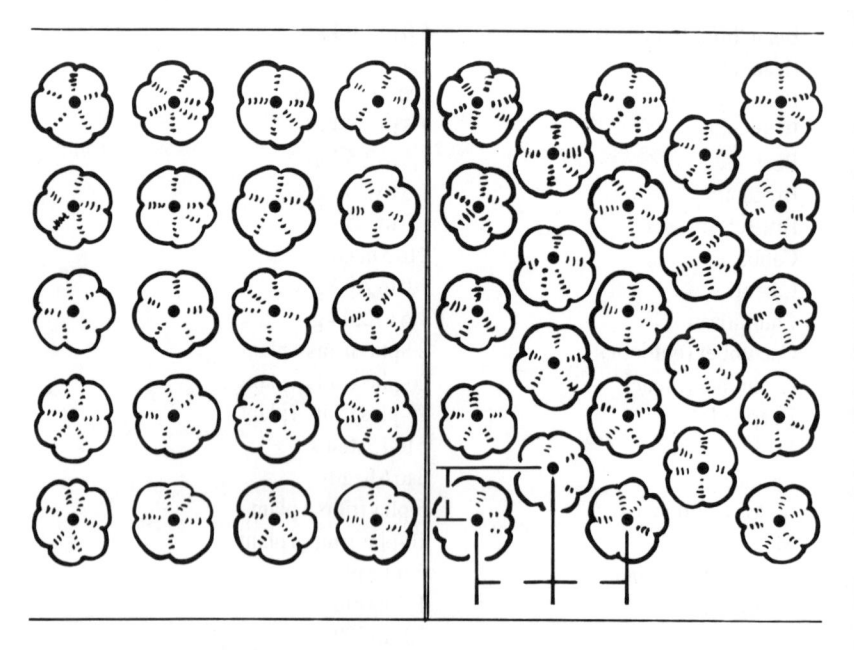

In the right-hand bed diagonal planting has increased the plant population, although a similar amount of space has been left between each plant as in the square-planted bed at left.

BASIC SOWING PERIODS

Because of the divergence of climates within each region, the sowing periods shown in the graph for each vegetable can give only a general guide to sowing times and should be adapted where necessary (see also 'Site and Climate').

BEAN, BROAD

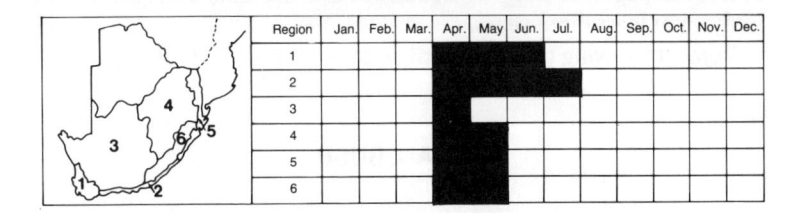

Region	Jan.	Feb.	Mar.	Apr.	May	Jun.	Jul.	Aug.	Sep.	Oct.	Nov.	Dec.
1												
2					■	■	■					
3					■							
4					■							
5					■							
6					■	■						

Unlike other beans, broad beans thrive in cool conditions and can withstand several degrees of frost although they may suffer a setback in severe frost conditions.

Yields of this deep-rooting vegetable will be dramatically increased if grown in deep-beds.

Soil: Use either 2:3:2 or 2:3:4 in the basic fertilizer prograqmme. A slightly acid soil between pH6,0 and 7,0 is preferred. If grown in strongly acid soils, pods may fail to form. The 25 g supplementary nitrogen side-dressing should be applied either when young plants are in vigorous growth or when flowering.

Succession: Two sowings, spaced a month apart, will extend the cropping season slightly.

Sow: Direct and do not transplant. Seed count — 65-150 seeds: 100 g.

Spacing guide: Conventional — rows 500 mm-1 m, and 200-300 mm within-row.
High density — 450-500 mm rows and 125 mm within-row. Double rows 250 mm apart and 250 mm within-row, with 600 mm-1 m between sets of double rows.

Harvest: Depending on growing conditions, harvesting should start 20 weeks plus from sowing. The cropping period is four weeks plus.

Pests and diseases: The two main problems are black aphids, easy to control, and rust, reasonably easy to control if treated at an early stage. Double rows are more difficult to control.

Points to watch: Flowers will not set in hot or very cold weather. Sowing out of the recommended sowing periods should be avoided because of frost or heat.

Provide supports for plants as they grow, to reduce the risk of wind or frost damage. Do not grow broad beans in the same soil, unless sterilised, for at least three years.

Remove growing tips at about 1 m to encourage pod setting.

BEAN, BUSH

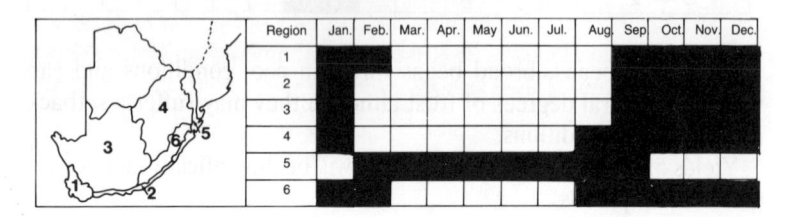

Region	Jan.	Feb.	Mar.	Apr.	May	Jun.	Jul.	Aug.	Sep.	Oct.	Nov.	Dec.
1												
2												
3												
4												
5												
6												

Bush beans, also called snap, dwarf or French, are easy to grow and have a short growing season.

Most cultivars are stringless, with very little tough fibre on the pod edges, unless overmature, and should snap in two when bent.

Bush beans are available as green-podded and yellow-podded, the latter often being referred to as wax beans. Unlike pole beans, bush beans are self-supporting and produce a heavy crop over a short period, making them suitable for succession sowing.

Soil: Use either 2:3:2 or 2:3:4 in the basic fertilizer programme. Plants grow well in moderately acid soil with a pH range of 5,5-6,5. The 50 g supplementary nitrogen side-dressing should be applied in two 25 g applications, first when flowering begins and again two weeks later. Some cultivars may produce excessive leaf growth if nitrogen is applied too early. The first application should then be given only when the first pods have set.

Succession: Sow at three-weekly intervals between August/September and November, fortnightly from then to January or February, depending on regional limitations. In region 5 fortnightly to three weekly sowings may be made between February and September.

Sow: Direct and do not transplant. Soil must be warm when sowing in spring. When seeds germinate the two large cotyledons — seed halves — must emerge without check. Gaps and yield losses can be considerable unless germination conditions are ideal. Seed count — 250-400 seeds: 100 g.

Spacing guide: Conventional — rows 450-900 mm and 75-100 mm within-row.
High density — 400 mm rows and 50 mm within-row, or broad-band at 150 mm square.

Harvest: Depending on growing conditions and cultivars, spring sowings should be ready for picking within 10 weeks from sowing, dropping to eight or nine weeks from summer sowings, rising again to 10 weeks from February sowings. The cropping period varies between two and six weeks. Peak yields are usually obtained from October and November sowings in most regions.

Pests and diseases: Possible pests and diseases are: aphids, bacterial blight, CMR beetle, plusia looper, red spider mite, rust and thrips.

Points to watch: Sowing in cold soils reduces germination. Sowing too deeply or too shallowly in hot weather and allowing soil to crust also affect germination. Avoid too much nitrogen, but ensure adequate soil fertility. Maintain constant soil moisture.

Infrequent harvesting reduces yields; regular picking every three to four days encourages new pod formation in younger plants. Harvest carefully to avoid loosening roots and do not pick beans when plants are wet.

BEAN, LIMA

Region	Jan.	Feb.	Mar.	Apr.	May	Jun.	Jul.	Aug	Sep.	Oct.	Nov.	Dec.
1									■	■		
2									■	■		
3									■	■		
4									■	■		
5										■		
6									■	■		

Lima beans are grown for green and dried shelled beans. In home gardens they are usually grown for immature green beans and are treated in the same way as broad beans — shelled when approaching maturity.

There are bush and pole cultivars, the bush ones being easier to grow than pole limas as they need no supporting, bear earlier and do not need such a long growing season.

In areas where broad beans are a 'hit-or-miss' crop, lima beans can be a superior substitute for freezing.

This is a vegetable worth considering for the home garden as the beans are not normally available in shops in fresh, canned or frozen forms. Seed sources are limited because of the relatively small commercial demand.

Lima beans have a distinctive chestnut flavour and pods usually contain three to four seeds.

Soil: Use either 2:3:2 or 2:3:4 in the basic fertilizer programme. Soil should be slightly acid, around pH6,5. The 50 g supplementary side-dressing, split into two 25 g applications, should be given three to five weeks after germination and when pods begin to set.

Succession: As lima beans have a long growing season and extended harvesting period, successional sowings are not necessary.

Sow: Direct and do not transplant. Lima beans are even more sensitive to cold soils than bush beans. Seed will not germinate if the soil temperature is below 15°C and at 20°C germination may take 14 days or longer. Seed count — 90-200 seeds: 100 g. Bush limas are larger seeded than pole types.

Spacing guide: Conventional — rows 600-900 mm and 100-200 mm within-row for bush limas: rows 900 mm-1,2 m and 200-300 mm within-row for pole cultivars.
Revised — rows 600 mm and 200 mm within-row for bush limas as they need adequate within-row space. Use the 200 mm within-row spacing for pole cultivars and the conventional row spacing.

Harvest: The first picking of bush limas should be 12-15 weeks from sowing. Pole limas will take one to two weeks longer. The cropping period for bush cultivars is eight weeks plus and pole limas will crop through to late autumn or early winter.

Pests and diseases: There are relatively few pests or diseases of this crop. Aphids, CMR beetle and plusia looper may occasionally cause some problems. Pre-emergence damping-off is likely if seed is sown in too cold soil.

Points to watch: Do not sow too early. Seed is brittle and damages easily, reducing germination. Maintain a uniform water supply throughout the growing season. Water requirements are critical at flowering stage.

Pod setting may stop in hot weather but will recommence when temperatures drop. Pick pods regularly to encourage new pod formation. Avoid loosening roots when picking and do not harvest when plants are wet. Do not sow too thickly.

BEAN, POLE

Region	Jan.	Feb.	Mar.	Apr.	May	Jun.	Jul.	Aug.	Sep.	Oct.	Nov.	Dec.
1	■								■	■	■	■
2									■	■	■	■
3									■	■	■	■
4									■	■	■	■
5		■	■	■	■	■	■					
6								■				

Pole beans are vines and must be provided with support on which to climb. Plants grow to a height of 2-3 m and, unless given adequate support, yields may be reduced.

This type of bean yields more heavily over a longer period than bush beans, and by growing vertically they are ideal for the smaller garden where it would not be practicable to make successive sowings of bush beans.

Experiments have shown that the old-established custom of spraying water on beans in hot weather to reduce flower drop is not effective. Some experiments indicated a decrease in yield when water sprayed compared with unsprayed plants. Flower drop can be reduced by ensuring good soil fertility and uniform soil moisture.

Soil: Conditions for optimum growth are similar to those of bush bean. Either of the recommended fertilizers may be used and the soil pH range is between 5,5 and 6,5. The two 25 g supplementary nitrogen side-dressings should be applied when pods start setting and three to four weeks later.

Succession: Although pole beans should have a long cropping period, the season can be extended, in most regions, with a mid- to late-September sowing and a second one in November or December. In region 5 pole bean sowing may be spaced four to eight weeks apart.

Sow: Direct and do not transplant. Soil must be warm when sowing in spring — a few degrees warmer than for bush beans. Seed count — 250-400 seeds: 100 g.

GROWING VEGETABLES

Spacing guide: Conventional — rows 600 mm-1,2 m and 150-250 mm within-row. Other systems are planting in hills and thinning to four to eight plants a hill, with a central pole and a pole for each plant with poles tied together at the top to give a tent-like appearance. Double rows about 300 mm apart and 150-250 mm within-row with poles tied together at the top are also common.

Pole beans are often grown in a circle with a central pole and a pole, wire or string for each plant, tied together to give a tent-like appearance.

Revised — Double rows 500-600 mm apart with 1 m between sets of double rows and 200-300 mm within-row. Single rows of 600 mm spacing and 150 mm within-row. Too-close spacing of double rows tends to reduce yields because of excessive shade on the inner sides.

Harvest: Cropping from a September sowing should start 10-14 weeks later, reducing to nine to 12 weeks from a November or December sowing. The cropping period is variable but six to nine weeks is a conservative average.

Pests and diseases: Watch for aphids, bacterial blight, CMR beetle, plusia looper, red spider mite, rust and thrips.

THE BASIC VEGETABLES

Points to watch: Avoid sowing in cold soil. Do not apply too much nitrogen when plants are young. Maintain uniform soil moisture throughout the growing period. Pick regularly and use firm supports. Birds may reduce yields by pecking out tender, young growing points. Bird netting may have to be used to enclose the plants completely.

BEET

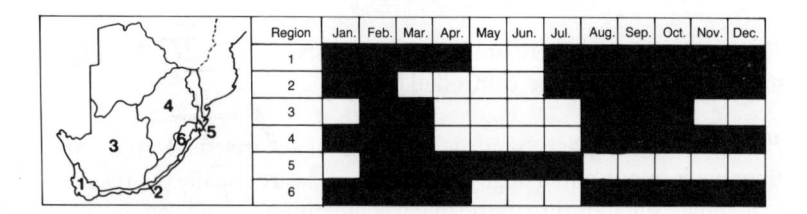

Region	Jan.	Feb.	Mar.	Apr.	May	Jun.	Jul.	Aug.	Sep.	Oct.	Nov.	Dec.
1												
2												
3												
4												
5												
6												

Beet, also known as beetroot or red beet, is a versatile vegetable: it may be eaten cooked, pickled, made into hot or cold soup and, if picked young, the baby beets need not be sliced or diced. Beet tops are also cooked as greens.

It is more susceptible to leaf disease than other root vegetables, however, and yields will suffer if plants are subjected to drought or low soil fertility.

Soil: In the basic fertilizer programme use 2:3:4 and aim for a soil pH of 6,0-7,0. A single 25 g supplementary nitrogen side dressing should be given four to six weeks from germination or when the roots show signs of swelling.

Succession: Small sowings every three to four weeks in spring and early summer and every four weeks from midsummer to autumn. Similar spaced sowings may be made during the optimum sowing period in region 5.

Sow: Direct is preferable, although small seedlings may be successfully transplanted if care is taken. Seed count — 400-1 000 seeds: 10 g.

Spacing guide: Conventional — rows 300-750 mm and 50-100 mm within-row.
High density — rows 150-175 mm and 50-100 mm within-row for small beets. Broad-band 50-100 mm each way with 500-700 mm between

bands. Rows 300 mm and 25-50 mm within-row for larger roots. If the plant population is too high, yields will be depressed.

Harvest: About 10 weeks from sowing under warm growing conditions and about eight weeks for baby beets. In colder periods it will take from 12 to 15 weeks to produce harvestable roots.

In warm weather the cropping period is about four weeks. In winter beet may be left in the soil for several weeks after reaching maturity without too much deterioration in texture and flavour.

Pests and diseases: There are no serious pests and diseases. Leaf spot may reduce yields unless controlled early.

Points to watch: Each 'seed' is a cluster of several seeds and early thinning is important. Tough and stringy roots are usually the result of inadequate soil moisture or too much competition. Avoid any checks in growth.

BROCCOLI

Region	Jan.	Feb.	Mar.	Apr.	May	Jun.	Jul.	Aug.	Sep.	Oct.	Nov.	Dec.
1	■	■										■
2		■										■
3		■										■
4		■	■									■
5	■	■	■	■								■
6	■	■										■

Broccoli, sometimes called calabrese and green sprouting broccoli, refers to the green or green-blue sprouting broccoli and not the winter-heading cauliflower called broccoli in Europe.

The edible head of broccoli is made up of unopen green or green-blue flower buds and thick fleshy stems. The central head at the top of the plant grows to a diameter of 150-250 mm or larger, and side-shoots which develop after the main head has been harvested grow to a 25 mm diameter or more.

It is a cool season crop, but is more tolerant of heat than most cauliflower cultivars and produces over a longer period.

Easy to grow, it is one of the more important autumn and winter crops where space is limited.

Soil: Broccoli and other brassicas are heavy feeders and must have a deep, fertile soil. Use 2:3:4 in the basic fertilizer programme and maintain a soil pH level of between 6,0 and 7,0. The first half of the 50 g supplementary nitrogen side-dressing should be applied four to six weeks after transplanting with the second 25 g after the central head has been harvested.

Succession: Two or three small seedbed sowings starting at the beginning of the recommended sowing period and at four-weekly intervals will extend the cropping period.

Sow: In seedbeds or seedtrays for transplanting. Sowings are made in the hottest months of the year and some light shading may be necessary. Shade should be removed 7-10 days before transplanting to ensure plants can adapt to garden conditions. Plants will be ready for transplanting four to six weeks from sowing. Seed count — 250-350 seeds: 1 g.

Spacing guide: Conventional — rows 500-900 mm and 300-600 mm within-row.
High density — rows 300 mm and 150 mm within-row; rows 450 mm and 100 mm within-row and 150 mm square. Side-shoot development is unlikely at these spacings. Square planting at 300 mm.
   High-density plantings give lower individual yields than wider-spaced plants and a shorter cropping period, but this is compensated by better quality heads and overall higher yields.

Harvest: Main heads, depending on the cultivar grown, are ready for harvesting nine weeks plus from transplanting. The cropping period is five weeks plus but less from high-density grown crops.

Pests and diseases: Aphids, bacterial spot, bagrada bug, larvae (caterpillars) of the diamond-back and greater cabbage moths, downy mildew and red spider mite. Seedlings may be killed by damping-off.

Points to watch: Do not let seedbeds or seedtrays dry out. Protect new transplants from sun for a few days. If aphids get into the central head or sideshoots they are almost impossible to kill.
   Too high temperatures may cause loose, uneven heads as well as leaf growth in the head. Severe frost can cause heads to decay. Hollow stem is caused by excessive growth, excessive heat, too much nitrogen or too wide spacings. Maintain regular, rapid growth otherwise yields may be reduced.

GROWING VEGETABLES

BRUSSELS SPROUTS

Region	Jan	Feb	Mar	Apr	May	Jun	Jul	Aug	Sep	Oct	Nov	Dec
1		■	■									
2		■	■	■								
3		■	■									
4		■	■	■								
5	■	■	■	■								
6		■	■	■								

One of the best winter vegetables as it produces small buds — sprouts — in the leaf axils from near ground level right up the stem over a long period.

Since the introduction of F_1 hybrid cultivars, growing Brussels sprouts is possible throughout Southern Africa in winter, even in subtropical areas, although results are not as good as in regions where cool to cold winters are experienced.

Soil: Requirements are similar to broccoli: a deep, fertile soil and a pH range of 6,0-7,0. Use 2:3:2 or 2:3:4 in the basic fertilizer programme. 2:3:4 is usually preferred.

Soil should be firm as plants can grow to 1 m tall and in strong winds there may be some root disturbance. In deep-beds, plants may need some supporting because of the looseness of the soil.

The 100 g supplementary nitrogen side-dressing should be split into two 50 g applications; the first four to six weeks from transplanting and the second when the first picking of sprouts is made.

Succession: Because of the long harvesting period, successional plantings are not necessary, but a sowing at either end of the recommended sowing period will extend harvesting by a few weeks.

Sow: In seedbeds or seedtrays for transplanting. Provide shade if necessary but not within seven days before transplanting. Shade for a few days after transplanting. Allow four to six weeks from sowing to transplanting. Seed count — 200-350 seeds: 1 g.

Spacing guide: Conventional — rows 500 mm-1 m and 350-600 mm within-row.
High density — for continuous cropping too high density planting is not recommended. Rows 750 mm and 600 mm within-row; square planting 500 mm up to 750 mm. The minimum spacing is 500 mm square otherwise yields may be depressed.

Harvest: Picking of the bottom sprouts should start about 13 weeks from transplanting, and the period of cropping, depending on plant growth, varies between 10 and 15 weeks.

Pests and diseases: Aphids, bacterial spot, bagrada bug, larvae of the diamond-back and greater cabbage moths, downy mildew, red spider mite and ring spot. Damping-off disease may attack overcrowded seedlings.

Points to watch: Regular spraying against the major pests. Too early sowings may result in blown (loose) sprouts. Extended periods of hot weather may stunt growth resulting in lower yields. Maintain regular and uniform soil moisture.

CABBAGE

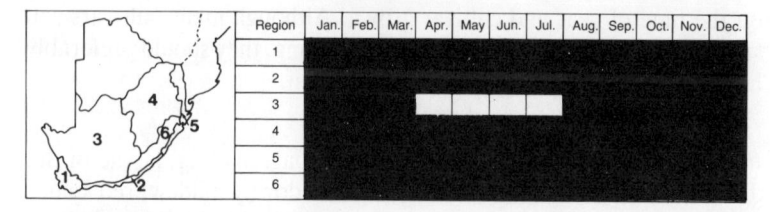

Cabbages can be successfully grown throughout the year in most parts of Southern Africa. The main requirements for continuity cropping are adequate space, careful selection of cultivars, and small but frequent plantings.

Like other brassicas — as members of the cabbage family are collectively called — cabbages are primarily cool season vegetables, but there are cultivars bred to withstand summer heat.

Soil: Being heavy feeders, cabbages need a deep, fertile soil with a pH between 6,0 and 7,0. Use 2:3:4 in the basic fertilizer programme as cabbages are heavy users of nitrogen and potash.

The supplementary side dressing of nitrogen, split into two 50 g applications, should be given about a month after transplanting and about four weeks later.

Succession: To maintain continuity, small sowings should be made every two to four weeks for warm weather harvesting. Four-weekly intervals should be adequate for cool weather cropping as heads remain firm longer.

Sow: In seedbeds or seedtrays for transplanting or direct in warm weather. Direct sowings in cold weather are not recommended as young plants may need too much attention to keep them growing. Allow 4-6 weeks from sowing to transplanting. Seed count — 200-400 seeds: 1 g.

Spacing guide: Conventional — rows 500-900 mm and 300-600 mm within-row, depending on the cultivar.

High-density — 250 mm square for small-heading cultivars, 350 mm square for small heads of larger-heading cabbages and 450 mm square for large heads.

If medium-sized heads are preferred for a single meal, the 350 mm square planting should be used as it gives a larger plant population in a given area. Diagonal planting may also be employed.

Harvest: From transplanting to harvest allow 10-15 weeks, depending on the time of year and cultivar grown. Although many cultivars will stand for a few weeks in winter before splitting, they should preferably be harvested as the heads enlarge and harden.

Pests and diseases: Aphids, bacterial spot, bagrada bug, larvae of the diamond-back and greater cabbage moths, downy mildew, red spider mite and damping-off of seedlings. Black rot may be a problem at times but there are disease-resistant cultivars.

A serious problem in many countries where brassicas are grown is clubroot, a fungus disease. It causes root swelling and eventual rotting. Since it was discovered in South Africa during the 1980s extra care must be taken when growing any of the cabbage family as there is no effective, long-lasting control. Spores can live in the soil for up to 20 years.

When clubroot is present the rotation period for brassicas should be 7-8 years or longer. Acid soils encourage clubroot development. A pH6,5 minimum may retard development of the disease.

Points to watch: Bolting — premature seed-stalk formation — may be caused by growing incorrect cultivars in a particular season. Maintain regular, uniform soil moisture. When heads start forming, the water requirement is higher.

Too much nitrogen early in winter may make the plants too tender to withstand severe frost. Space sowings correctly to avoid gluts in summer and shortages in the longer-growing winter period.

CARROT

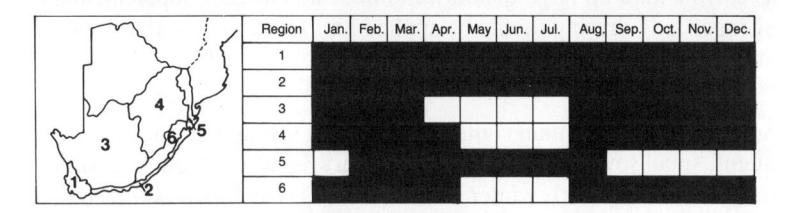

Region	Jan.	Feb.	Mar.	Apr.	May	Jun.	Jul.	Aug.	Sep.	Oct.	Nov.	Dec.
1												
2												
3					☐	☐	☐					
4				☐	☐		☐	☐				
5	☐	☐							☐	☐	☐	☐
6				☐	☐							

Carrots are one of the easiest vegetables to grow. They are adaptable and grow under a wide range of conditions, although they prefer mild temperatures — neither too hot nor too cold.

This vegetable is tolerant of mismanagement and is not particularly susceptible to pests and diseases. Carrots can be harvested throughout the year with only basic attention.

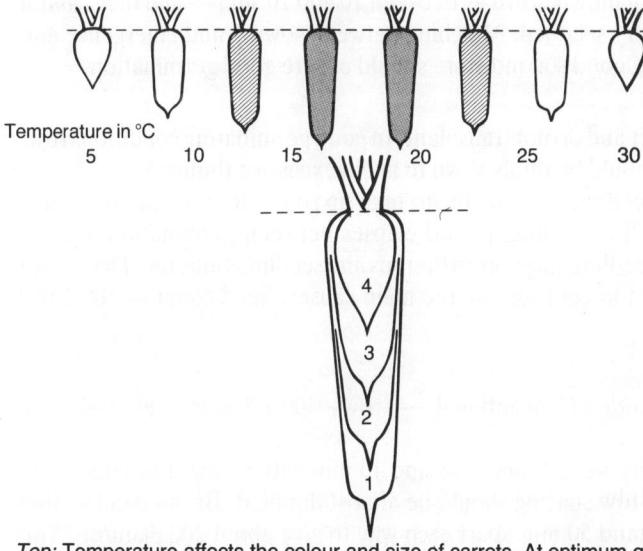

Temperature in °C
5   10   15   20   25   30

Top: Temperature affects the colour and size of carrots. At optimum growing temperatures colour and size development is good, but both deteriorate with extremes of temperature.

Above, centre: Carrots develop from the shoulder downwards. Under ideal growing temperatures and conditions full-sized roots (1) should be obtained. As temperatures fluctuate, the recognised size and shape of a cultivar may vary considerably (2, 3 or 4).

Soils, lack of water, or insufficient fertility may also affect size and colour.

Soil: Soils known to be infested with nematodes (eelworm) should be avoided. A slightly acid soil is required in the range of pH6,0-6,5.

The 2:3:4 fertilizer should be used in the basic fertilizer programme as carrots take up large quantities of potash. The 25 g supplementary nitrogen side-dresing should be applied four to six weeks after germination.

Succession: To maintain continuity cropping throughout the year, frequent, small sowings should be made every 3-4 weeks from late winter to late autumn or early winter in warmer areas. The final sowings before winter should be doubled to provide extra roots to cover the non-sowing period. In some areas of region 5 sowings may be restricted to late summer through to spring.

When late winter sowings are made, seed should be sown thicker than normal as germination may be affected by cold soils. Some form of mulching will help germination in cold weather.

Midsummer sowings may also result in poor germination as seeds should be shallowly sown — between 10 and 20 mm — and they cannot tolerate a dry seedbed. Mulching between sowing and emergence and maintaining good soil moisture should ensure good germination.

Sow: Direct and do not transplant. In good germinating conditions rows or bands should be thinly sown to avoid excessive thinning.

Carrot seedlings are unable to take up soil nutrients until root hairs form and, if a too long period elapses between germination and the root-hair seedling stage, growth stops and seedlings may die. Drying out of soil and too cold soil are the main causes. Seed count — 500-1 000 seeds: 1 g.

Spacing guide: Conventional — rows 400-700 mm and 25-75 mm within-row.
High density — 150 mm rows and 40 mm within-row. For large roots the within-row spacing should be almost doubled. Broad-band — thin plants to stand 50 mm apart each way to give about 200 plant/m^2. This spacing will give medium-sized roots. A 75 mm spacing will give more than 150 larger roots to a square metre.

Harvest: From sowing to harvest in warmer weather, early cultivars may be harvested at a young stage 8-10 weeks from sowing. In winter, depending on the cultivar, the period may extend up to 20 weeks for mature roots. The harvesting period also varies according to the season. In warm periods from 3-5 weeks but longer in winter, as roots may be left in the ground without too much deterioration.

Pests and diseases: There are no serious pests of carrots. Alternaria can kill off leaves, and in warm, humid conditions with high-density sowings the disease may spread rapidly unless controlled in time. Some cultivars are more tolerant of alternaria than others.

Seedlings may be attacked by grasshoppers and beetles and damping-off may occur in too-thick seedling stands.

Points to watch: Maintain constant soil moisture from sowing to emergence. Do not water too heavily after emergence otherwise roots will not penetrate to deeper levels. When roots are swelling, give deep waterings. Avoid too thick sowings. Yields may vary if optimum temperatures are not maintained. Above and below the optimum range, root size is usually smaller.

CAULIFLOWER

Cauliflower is the most difficult brassica to grow successfully. Soil conditions need to be almost perfect, the climate must be cool, and plants must never receive any check in growth from germination through to head formation.

Because of its precise needs, the choice of cultivars is important as a few are less demanding than others.

Soil: Plants are gross feeders and need high soil fertility from transplanting through to harvest. The soil pH range is between 6,0 and 7,0.

The fertilizer in the basic fertilizer programme should preferably be 2:3:4. The split supplementary nitrogen side-dressing of 50 g at each application should be given a month after transplanting and about a month later.

Some soils may also need trace elements — magnesium, manganese, boron and molybdenum — if soils are too acid for optimum growth.

A nitrogen deficiency shows with leaf yellowing and may cause buttoning — premature head formation. Pithy cores and discoloured, deformed heads are symptoms of boron deficiency. In magnesium- and manganese-deficient soils older leaves lose the green colouring apart from the veins. Malformation of the growing point of young plant, together with long, strap-like leaves indicates a shortage of molybdenum.

Foliar spraying with a trace element mixture containing these elements, together with a spreader-sticker, could correct the problem if tackled in time but, more likely, the damage will have been done.

Succession: Sowings every 3-4 weeks through the sowing season will provide continuity cropping from late autumn to late winter or early spring if combined with early, mid- and late-maturing cultivars.

Sow: In seedbeds or seedtrays for transplanting. Avoid any check in growth. Sowings made between December and February should be ready for transplanting 4-6 weeks later. A March sowing may require an extra week. Seed count — 200-400 seeds: 1 g.

Spacing guide: Conventional — rows 600-900 mm and 350-600 mm within row.
High density — small cultivars 500 mm square, medium-sized cultivars 650 mm square and 750 mm square for large-heading cultivars. If large-headed cultivars are planted closer than 750 mm square, head size will be reduced but overall yields may be similar or higher.

Harvest: Early F_1 cultivars can produce heads 7-10 weeks from transplanting; midseason ones take 12-15 weeks while late cultivars take 20 weeks or longer from an autumn planting. Heads must be harvested as they approach maturity.

Pests and diseases: Aphids, bacterial spot, bagrada bug, larvae of the diamond-back and greater cabbage moths, downy mildew, red spider mite and damping-off of seedlings.

Points to watch: Buttoning may be caused by insufficient water, lack of nitrogen, too low or too high temperatures, wind and a general lack of soil fertility. Blindness — no growing point — may be caused by mechanical damage, cutworm damage or adverse temperatures. Whiptail — deformed leaves and die-back of the growing point — is associated with strongly acid soils lacking in available molybdenum. Discoloured heads are usually the result of poor protection from the sun. Maintain constant soil moisture.

CUCUMBER

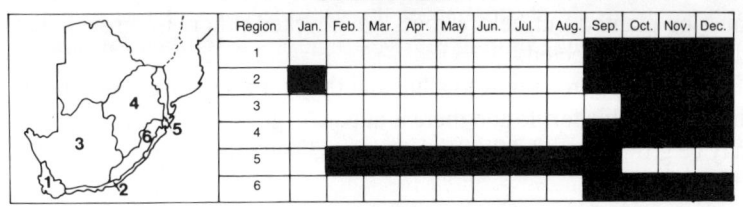

Region	Jan.	Feb.	Mar.	Apr.	May	Jun.	Jul.	Aug.	Sep.	Oct.	Nov.	Dec.
1								■	■	■	■	■
2		■						■	■	■	■	■
3								■		■	■	■
4								■	■	■	■	■
5	■	■	■	■	■	■			■	■	■	■
6								■	■	■	■	■

There are two main types of cucumber grown in home gardens — those usually grown in tunnels or greenhouses known as English, European, tunnel, greenhouse or hothouse cucumbers, and the outdoor type referred to as cucumber or ridge cucumber. In between there are hybrid cultivars suitable for both indoor and outdoor growing.

Cucumbers should be trained up supports for maximum plant population in a given area.

Although commercial growers seldom mix cucumbers and tomatoes in tunnels, home gardeners can and do get good crops of both when grown together in a domestic tunnel or greenhouse if a little extra care is taken.

Soil: Cucumbers respond to large amounts of organic matter, preferably well-rotted manure. To ensure plants take full advantage of the manure, work it into the soil in a concentrated area where seeds are to be sown in individual bowls (hills). Soils should be moderately acid between pH5,5 and 6,5.

In the basic fertilizer programme use 2:3:2 — too much potash may slow down the essential rapid growth of plants in the early stages.

The split supplementary nitrogen side-dressing — 50 g equally divided — should be given when plants start forming fruits and 3-4 weeks later.

Tunnel-grown cucumbers should not be grown in the same soil year after year otherwise there may be a build up of soil diseases. If it is impracticable to sterilise soil, use grow-bags, large planting bags, or 350 mm-diameter plastic pots with either a sterilised soil mix or a soil-less growing medium. A different approach to feeding will be required for container-grown plants based on one or other of the hydroponic chemical mixtures.

Cucumbers have large root systems and require slow, deep waterings. Plants temporarily stop growing if there is inadequate water in the soil or growing medium.

Succession: Well-grown plants have a relatively long cropping season. The period may be extended by two or more spaced sowings through the recommended sowing period.

GROWING VEGETABLES

Sow: Preferably direct. If seeds are sown in small planting bags, they must be planted out before roots are checked otherwise growth and yields will be affected.

Sow two or three seeds to a hill and thin out to the strongest one. If the soil is highly fertile and there is adequate growing space, two plants may be grown in each hill. Seed count — 30-40 seeds: 1 g.

Spacing guide: Conventional — 1,0-1,8 m rows and 300 mm within-row for single plants. Bowls (hills) are spaced 600 mm to 1 m apart. Two plants to a grow-bag.

Tunnel-grown cucumbers are usually pruned and spaced 300-400 mm apart.

Harvest: Cropping should start 8-10 weeks from sowing. The harvesting period varies according to the type of cucumber, the growing environment — tunnel, greenhouse or outdoors — and the cultivar, between six and eight weeks. Similarly, the number of fruits harvested is also variable.

Pests and diseases: The main pests and disease are: Anthracnose, aphids, downy and powdery mildew, fruit (pumpkin) flies, red spider mite and thrips. Plants attacked by mosaic virus should be removed and destroyed.

Points to watch: Most hothouse hybrid cultivars are either all female — producing only female flowers, so eliminating the risk of pollination — or mainly female — producing a few male flowers on the lower axils of the main stem. Male flowers should be removed before they open, otherwise pollinated fruits may be misshapen and bitter. Female flowers are identified by the small, immature fruit behind the flower.

Most outdoor cultivars need to be pollinated to set fruit. It is usual for this type to produce male flowers first followed about a week later by female flowers.

Tunnel-grown cucumbers will give better yields if the water they receive is stored in the tunnel before use, as cucumber roots are susceptible to low temperatures.

Thinning may be necessary to restrict the number of fruits on a plant at any one time. Usually too many female flowers are formed on hothouse cultivars.

Most hothouse cucumbers produce more and better fruits on laterals — sideshoots — than from the main stem. After fruits set on laterals, pruning of further lateral growth must be done if plants are closely spaced. If there is adequate space, the growing point may be removed when a plant has four true leaves and the sideshoots are then trained as leaders.

In hot weather shade will be necessary for tunnel cucumbers, preferably not from the plant's leaf canopy as too much foliage can depress yields.

Cucumbers require high humidity in tunnels otherwise leaves turn brown and die. However, spraying foliage to create humidity increases the risk of foliar diseases, so that it is best to water the paths and surrounding areas. The high humidity required by cucumbers may be a limiting factor when growing tomatoes in the same environment.

Powdery mildew is a devastating disease and unless controlled will quickly kill plants. The white powdery spores spread rapidly under tunnel and greenhouse environments.

Harvest every two to four days, as soon as fruits are large enough to use. Fruits must not mature on the vines otherwise new flowers may not form or younger fruits may become misshapen. Cold conditions may also cause misshapen fruits.

Avoid watering the base of plants — the main stem — as it may cause rotting. Some form of collar around the stem or ridging up to provide rapid drainage away from the stem is recommended.

In hot weather plants may wilt during the day even though there is adequate soil moisture, but always check on the water content if wilting occurs.

EGGPLANT

The eggplant, also known as aubergine, bringal (brinjal) or eggfruit, is related to the tomato, pepper and potato. It is a subtropical plant highly susceptible to cold and needs a long growing season of warm weather.

Soil: The combination of being a gross feeder and the long-growing season makes a highly fertile soil a prerequisite for successful growing. Use 2:3:4 in the basic fertilizer programme. Soil pH should be in the 5,5-6,5 range.

The split 50 g supplementary nitrogen side-dressing should be given when plants set the first fruits and the second 25 g a month later.

Deep watering is essential. In deep-beds and containers plants may need supporting as they often become top heavy with large numbers of fruits, and root damage by rocking may otherwise occur.

Succession: Successional sowings are not necessary.

Sow: In seedtrays, preferably with bottom heat in late winter and early spring. Protection from cold is essential. Eggplants are more susceptible to cold than tomatoes and must not receive any growth check. Six to 10 weeks is needed to grow them to transplant size from sowing. Growth from then on must be rapid and uninterrupted otherwise plants will be stunted, hard and woody.

Small seedlings with two to four true leaves should be planted out from the seedtray into pots or small planting bags and grown on until ready for planting in the garden.

Eggplants are usually planted out about two weeks later than tomatoes in spring when soil and air temperatures are warm. Seed count — 170-250 seeds: 1 g.

Spacing guide: Conventional — rows 700-900 mm and 450-750 mm within-row.
High density — rows 700-750 mm and 450-500 mm within-row.

Harvest: The first fruits — half to three-quarter grown — should be ready for cutting about 12 weeks from transplanting, depending on the growing conditions. The average harvest period is between eight and 10 weeks but may continue through to early winter, the first frost or cold spell.

Pests and diseases: There are no serious pests and diseases. Wilt diseases cannot be controlled and infected plants should be removed and destroyed. Blossom-end rot may occur. Early and late blight can attack plants. Sunscald of fruits is possible under hot, dry conditions if fruits are exposed. Possible pests are aphids and red spider mite.

Points to watch: Always cut fruits with a sharp knife. Support heavily laden branches. Do not plant out too early. Harvest while fruits are glossy skinned. A test for picking is to press the side of the fruit with the thumb; if at the right picking stage — not overmature — the indentation will not last.

THE BASIC VEGETABLES
LEEK

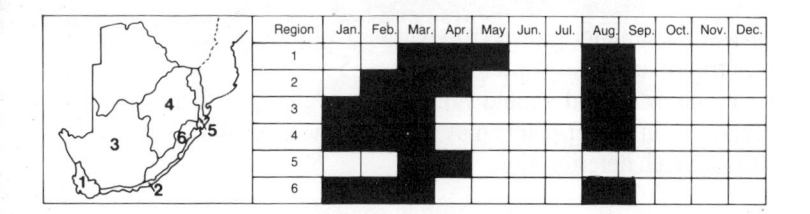

Region	Jan.	Feb.	Mar.	Apr.	May	Jun.	Jul.	Aug.	Sep.	Oct.	Nov.	Dec.
1								■				
2			■	■				■				
3			■	■	■			■				
4			■		■	■		■				
5			■		■			■				
6			■	■				■				

Leeks have a mild onion flavour and are one of the most versatile vegetables for the garden and home. They are primarily a winter vegetable although they grow quite well in heat.

They are grown for the blanched leaf stems, many leaf bases wrapped around each other, as the leek does not form a bulb like the onion. Blanching is usually done by planting in a 150 mm deep trench, gradually filled in as the plant grows, then earthing the soil up around the stems as they develop.

Extremes of temperature may induce bolting, slow growth and toughness.

Soil: A slightly acid to neutral soil is needed, between pH6,5 and 7,0, the nearer 7,0 the better. Quality of the blanched leaf stems is directly linked to the degree of soil fertility. Either of the fertilizers may be used in the basic fertilizer programme. The split supplementary nitrogen side-dressing should be applied about a month after planting and a month later — 25 g each time.

Succession: Continuity sowings may be made during the optimum period in summer for winter cropping but should be limited to one or two sowings between July, under some protection and warmth, and August. Leeks grow quite well in heat if given a cool start in spring.

Sow: In seedbeds or seedtrays for transplanting. Direct sowings may be made but then trenching is not possible. The period between sowing and transplanting varies according to the season. In late winter and early spring allow 8-10 weeks to reach transplantable size. A summer sowing will take 6-8 weeks. Seed count — 250 to 400 seeds: 1 g.

Spacing guide: Conventional — rows 300-900 mm, depending on whether ridging is to be done, and 75-150 mm within-row.
High density — rows 300 mm and 100 mm within-row or 450 mm rows

and 50 mm within-row; square planting between 100 and 150 mm. Deep mulching will assist blanching.

Harvest: A summer-grown crop will be ready to harvest 11-15 weeks from transplanting. A winter crop takes 15 weeks or longer. In summer the cropping period should not be extended beyond three or four weeks, but in winter plants may be left in the ground for much longer without much deterioration.

Pests and diseases: There are no serious pests or diseases.

Points to watch: Lift leeks carefully otherwise the root base may be ripped off. To clean leeks, put them into clean water upside down to remove soil and grit from between the leaves. Plant deeper than onions, almost to where the leaves divide. Don't start blanching — earthing up — too early otherwise plants may rot if soil is ridged into the open leaves and covers the growing point.

LETTUCE

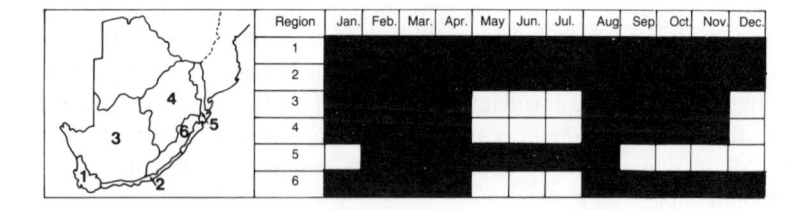

Lettuce is one of the most important and popular vegetables because it is the basis of fresh salads, has a pleasant taste and has a low kilojoule (calorie) value. It is easy to prepare for eating and just as easy to grow.

With careful planning, lettuce can be available the year round in most regions without taking up too much space — a few plants from each sowing will keep an average-sized family supplied as and when needed.

There are four basic types of lettuce: crisphead, butterhead, looseleaf and cos or romaine. Crisphead lettuce are the most popular in Southern Africa. Heads are firm and hard and the texture is brittle and crisp. Head size is usually large, 150 mm diameter plus, and often has a mass in excess of 1 kg.

Butterhead lettuce are smaller, softer, more fragile and perishable than crispheads and have loosely folded, thicker leaves of a buttery texture. They are superior for tossed salads.

Looseleaf lettuce form clusters of partially open leaves. They are grown as a 'cut-and-come-again' lettuce and, because they have less exacting growth requirements than head-forming kinds, can be used to fill in production gaps.

Cos lettuce have a more upright growth habit with a long head, if formed, with long, narrow spatulate leaves. If heads form, they are self-closing with leaves curling inwards at the tips. Leaves appear coarse but are tender and sweet and damage easily. They are usually grown during cooler months.

Lettuce is basically a cool-weather vegetable, but summer, heat-resisting cultivars reduce the problem of harvesting gaps.

Soil: Lettuce performs poorly in strongly acid soils. The optimum pH range is between 6,5 and 7,0.

Although lettuce is not a heavy feeder, it needs constant nutrients and moisture because its root system is shallow and poor. If too much manure is used in warm weather, plants may develop loose heads and bolt.

Manure and compost should be shallowly dug in before sowing or planting.

Lettuce take up most of their soil nutrients between 14 and 21 days before harvest, so there must be adequate nutrients and moisture towards the end of the growing period.

Use 2:3:2 in the basic fertilizer programme. The split 50 g supplementary nitrogen side-dressing should be given about 5-6 weeks before harvesting starts and 3-4 weeks later, 25 g at each application. Maintain constant soil moisture in the top 200-300 mm of soil.

Succession: Small sowings every 2-3 weeks in early spring, then fortnightly between October and February and thereafter every 2-3 weeks in the recommended sowing period should ensure continuity even through the non-sowing winter months, if different kinds and cultivars are used. Continuity problems are more acute in parts of region 5.

Sow: Direct in hot weather as transplanting may be difficult. Direct or seedbeds or seedtrays at other times. Seed will not germinate if soil temperatures are too high. The maximum soil temperature for germinating butterhead lettuce is 25°C, while crispheads may germinate at three to five degrees higher.

Research indicates that afternoon sowing is preferable to morning: the temperature-sensitive part of germination takes place at night when soil temperatures are lower.

Constant moisture will keep down soil temperatures. Fluid sowing of pre-germinated seeds also overcomes the germination in heat problem. Another way to overcome thermo-dormancy — that is, no germination until the soil cools — is to place seed in water in a domestic refrigerator at about 5°C and allow it to imbibe for up to 48 hours, then mix the seed with dry sand and sow immediately.

The time from sowing to transplanting depends on the time of year: in warm weather, 3-4 weeks; in cooler weather 4-6 weeks. Seed count — 600-1 000 seeds: 1 g.

Spacing guide: Conventional — crisphead, rows 450-600 mm and 250-400 mm within-row. Butterhead and cos, rows 300-350 mm and 250 mm within-row; looseleaf, rows 300-400 mm and 100-300 mm within-row.
High density — crisphead, rows 400-450 mm and 250-300 mm within-row; butterhead and cos, 200-300 mm square; looseleaf, rows 125-150 mm and 25-50 mm within-row.

Harvest: Summer-grown crops, depending on the type and cultivar, will be ready for harvesting 10-14 weeks from sowing, seven weeks plus from transplanting. Looseleaf lettuce should be ready after 5-7 weeks, while still small, with a second cut 3-4 weeks later. Alternatively, looseleaf lettuce leaves may be taken from the plant as and when required.

In winter, allow at least 15 weeks from sowing and 7-10 weeks from transplanting. Harvest as heads approach maturity.

Pests and diseases: There are few serious pests and diseases. Maturing heads may rot from the base under warm, humid conditions. Aphids may be a problem occasionally. Lettuce mosaic, a virus spread by aphids or seed, cannot be controlled in the garden. Seed of some cultivars is mosaic tested.

Points to watch: No germination in heat may mean harvesting gaps. Using thinnings may help in staggered plantings if successfully transplanted. Choose cultivars for the appropriate season. Thin early and re-thin if necessary to recommended within-row spacings. Protect against severe frost in winter and provide light shade in the heat of summer.

MELON

Region	Jan.	Feb.	Mar.	Apr.	May	Jun.	Jul.	Aug.	Sep.	Oct.	Nov.	Dec.
1									■	■	■	
2									■	■		
3									■			
4								■	■			
5					■	■	■					
6								■	■	■	■	

Melons, also known as muskmelons, sweet melons and sometimes cantaloupes, are one of the more exotic crops grown by gardeners, although they are not easy to grow in all areas.

Gardeners with tunnels or greenhouses are likely to have more success than those who grow them outdoors, although earlier-maturing cultivars with more disease resistance have made melon growing easier. Some cultivars have been bred for tunnel and greenhouse growing, the majority are outdoor ones, while a few are dual purpose.

Soil: Melons respond to large quantities of organic matter in the soil and, if grown in hills, manure can be concentrated beneath the growing area. Soil should be slightly acid in the pH6,0-7,0 range.

In the basic fertilizer programme use 2:3:2 in preference to 2:3:4. The supplementary nitrogen side-dressing should be split into two 25 g applications, the first when fruits begin to form and the second 3-4 weeks later.

Tunnel-grown melons should not be grown in the same soil in successive years as there may be a disease build-up. Melons, like cucumbers, may be grown in containers in sterilised soil or a soilless growing medium. Feeding container-grown plants differs from plants grown in prepared soil and regular feeding with a hydroponic solution or powder at the rate recommended for each product will supply the plants' needs.

Melons have large root systems and need a constant moisture supply otherwise they stop growing temporarily, wilt and yields may be reduced.

Succession: Melons have a long growing season and a single sowing is normal. A second sowing may be made towards the end of the recommended sowing period, but in many areas a late sowing is more prone to pest and disease attacks and harvesting may be curtailed by cold weather.

Sow: Direct. If seeds are sown in small planting bags they must not receive any growth check otherwise yields will be adversely affected.

If sown in a hill, early thinning to one strong-growing plant is important to avoid root disturbance. Seed count — 35-45 seeds: 1 g.

Spacing guide: Conventional — rows 1,2-2,5 m and 300-900 mm within-row. Hills 1-1,5 m apart.
High density — 300-400 mm between plants, pruned and trained up supports.

Harvest: Picking should begin 12-16 weeks from an outdoor sowing and 1-3 weeks earlier in tunnels. The cropping period varies according to the cultivar and system of growing. Outdoor melons should produce five or more fruits over a 6-8 week period. Tunnel cultivars should give double the outdoor-grown yield over 8-10 weeks. Numbers of fruits harvested may vary considerably.

Pests and diseases: Anthracnose, aphids, downy and powdery mildew, fruit (pumpkin) flies, red spider mite and thrips.

Points to watch: When plants have developed 5-7 leaves, the growing point is removed to encourage laterals (sideshoots) to form. Three to four are retained and trained up a trellis or some other suitable support. In tunnels they are usually trained laterally on wires.

Male flowers must not be removed as they are needed to pollinate female ones.

If tunnel temperatures exceed 35°C, bees will not be active and fruit setting may be affected. Hand pollination may be necessary in tunnels and greenhouses to get a good fruit set if there is insufficient bee and insect activity because of heat or screening.

Avoid overwatering when fruits are ripening otherwise splitting may occur. Melons are vine-ripe when the stems break away as fruits are lifted. Fruits are likely to be heavy and, when swelling, will need some form of support.

Excess fruits should be removed if too many set at any one time, otherwise the size may be reduced as well as the chances of further fruit setting.

Provide shade for tunnel-grown plants, preferably shade cloth as a too-large leaf canopy reduces yields.

Plants need high humidity, particularly in tunnels and greenhouses. Avoid spraying or misting foliage; do not water the base of the stem and give each plant a collar at soil level to reduce the risk of water collecting, or ridge up around the stem to drain away the water.

NEW ZEALAND SPINACH

Region	Jan.	Feb.	Mar.	Apr.	May	Jun.	Jul.	Aug.	Sep.	Oct.	Nov.	Dec.
1												
2											■	■
3										■	■	■
4			■	■	■	■	■	■	■	■	■	■
5			■	■	■	■	■	■	■	■	■	■
6										■	■	■

New Zealand spinach is not a true spinach, but the leaves are used as a spinach substitute.

It thrives in heat, is slow to bolt and produces masses of leaves in summer when spinach cannot be grown. The plant is large and forms a dense ground cover and, in areas where it is not killed off in winter, may become invasive.

Soil: Soil pH should be between 6,0 and 7,0. Either of the fertilizers may be used in the basic fertilizer programme. The 100 g supplementary nitrogen side-dressing is applied in two stages — 50 g a month after germination, when the plants are growing vigorously and the second 50 g 4-6 weeks later.

Succession: The plant has a long productive life throughout summer and continuity sowings are unnecessary.

Sow: Direct or transplant. Seed is sometimes difficult to germinate. Soak seeds in warm water for 2-3 hours before sowing. Seed count — 10-15 seeds: 1 g.

Spacing guide: Conventional-rows 600 mm-1,5 m and 450-500 mm within-row.

Harvest: Picking begins about 10 weeks from sowing and continues throughout summer until frost.

Pests and diseases: There are no serious pests and diseases. Rust may occasionally be a problem.

Points to watch: Regular picking of up to two-thirds of the branch tips will encourage new growth.

Plants usually self-seed and young plants may be potted up and grown through winter if protected against frost.

If plants become too dense, they should be chopped back as rotting may otherwise occur near soil level.

GROWING VEGETABLES

ONION

Region	Jan.	Feb.	Mar.	Apr.	May	Jun.	Jul.	Aug.	Sep.	Oct.	Nov.	Dec.
1					■							
2					■							
3					■							
4				■								
5				■								
6				■								

Onions grown for dry bulbs are in the soil for up to six months from transplanting for short-day cultivars and even longer for long-day ones, which is restricting where garden space is at a premium.

Another factor to consider is the poor keeping quality of most short-day cultivars.

Onions can also be temperamental. Some years good bulbs are produced; in other years, with less favourable growing conditions, much of the crop may produce thick necks and bolters.

Photoperiodism — the growth response of a plant to the length of day, or more correctly, to the length of light and dark periods — has, together with temperature, a considerable effect on onion bulbing.

There are so-called short-day cultivars, grown mainly above a line passing through Durban, Bloemfontein and Port Nolloth, and long-day cultivars grown south of the line. Long-day cultivars should not be grown north of the line as they often fail to produce satisfactory bulbs.

Bulb onions are grown through the winter, because changes in light and dark periods control the initiation of the bulbing process and also because plants need cool weather for early growth — tops and feeding roots — warm weather for bulb formation, and even warmer weather to mature the bulbs.

Soil: Onions are one of the heaviest feeding vegetables and must have a highly fertile soil throughout the growing period. Soil pH should be between 6,0 and 6,5 as yields may be reduced in strongly acid or alkaline soils.

The basic fertilizer programme should be adjusted for this crop. The superphosphate application remains the same, but the 2:3:4 fertilizer should be increased from 100 g/m^2 to 150 g.

Onions must have adequate nitrogen in winter to reduce the risk of bolting. Excessive nitrogen may induce too much vegetative growth and thick necks will develop.

The split supplementary nitrogen side-dressing should be adequate if applied at 25 g 5-7 weeks after transplanting and again 4-6 weeks later.

THE BASIC VEGETABLES

Onions take 7–10 weeks to reach transplanting size — about 150 mm long. To make transplanting easier, both leaf tips and roots may be slightly trimmed. It is important to transplant at the same depth as the plants grew in the seedbed; too deep planting may inhibit bulb development.

Succession: Bulb onions are not grown for succession.

Sow: Seedbed sowing for transplanting. Direct sowings may be made but add to the length of time plants occupy a bed.

Allow 7-10 weeks from sowing to transplanting. Transplanting depth

GROWING VEGETABLES

should not be more than plants grow in the seedbed. Too deep planting may inhibit bulb development, particularly in soils with a tendency to compact. Seed count — 200-350 seeds: 1 g.

Spacing guide: Conventional — rows 400-600 mm and 25-100 mm within-row.
High density — rows 300 mm and 40-50 mm within-row. Rows 300 mm and 25 mm within-row for medium-sized bulbs.

Harvest: Depending on cultivars, harvesting of short-day onions starts 25-30 weeks from transplanting and about 35 weeks for long-day ones.

Pests and diseases: Main pests and diseases are thrips, purple (alternaria) blotch, downy mildew and white bulb rot. There are no registered home-garden controls for purple blotch or white bulb rot.

Alternaria blotch causes uneven blotches on onion foliage. Later, leaves turn brown and progressively die back.

Points to watch: Maintain high fertility and a good balance of nitrogen. Constant soil moisture until tops turn yellow and topple. Watering is most critical when bulbs start enlarging. Choose suitable cultivars for the region.

THE BASIC VEGETABLES

PARSLEY

Region	Jan.	Feb.	Mar.	Apr.	May	Jun.	Jul.	Aug.	Sep.	Oct.	Nov.	Dec.
1												
2												
3												
4												
5												
6												

Parsley is one of the most important herbs and is also a basic vegetable because of its many and varied uses.

It is hardy to cold although foliage may be killed off in severe frost unless protected, or a frost-hardy winter cultivar is grown. It is sensitive to heat and under hot, dry conditions foliage may become coarse and tough.

Soil: A slightly acid soil, pH6,0-7,0 is preferred. Use the basic fertilizer programme, either 2:3:2 or 2:3:4, when preparing the bed. The supplementary nitrogen side-dressing should be applied at 50 g a month after germination and another 50 g a month later or split into four 25 g applications a month after emergence and then at 3-4 weekly intervals.

Succession: Spring and autumn sowings should provide year-round continuity. Parsley should be treated as an annual as it may become coarse or run to seed in the second year.

Sow: Direct or transplant. Seeds are slow to germinate and should be soaked in warm water for 24 hours immediately before sowing. Radish seeds, sown with parsley, will indicate where the parsley seedlings will eventually emerge. Seed should not be sown deeper than 5-10 mm and constant soil moisture must be maintained. Seed count — 400-700 seeds: 1 g.

Spacing guide: Conventional — rows 350-500 mm and 100-200 mm within-row.
High density — 200 mm square.

Harvest: In summer cropping starts 12-14 weeks from sowing. An autumn sowing will be 1-2 weeks later.

Pests and diseases: There are no serious pests or diseases.

GROWING VEGETABLES

A late-winter or early spring sowing and another, using a winter cultivar, in mid to late summer should ensure a year-round supply of parsley, by using only a small corner of the garden.

Points to watch: Avoid unnecessary cultivation around plants as they are delicate and easily damaged. Regular cropping will encourage new growth.

PARSNIP

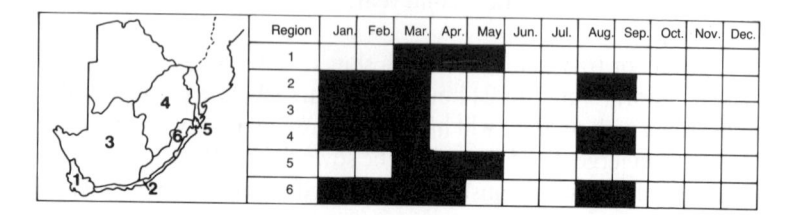

Region	Jan.	Feb.	Mar.	Apr.	May	Jun.	Jul.	Aug.	Sep.	Oct.	Nov.	Dec.
1												
2	■	■	■					■	■			
3	■	■	■					■	■			
4	■	■	■					■	■			
5		■	■	■								
6	■	■	■	■				■	■			

Parsnips are not among the most popular vegetables. Some of the reasons are: they have a long growing season, many people do not know them or how to use them, germination is unpredictable, the sweet, nutty flavour is not always appreciated, but they are an excellent winter vegetable as they may be used in various ways.

Soil: Deep soils are preferable as roots penetrate to a considerable depth when not restricted. Soils should be slightly acid, pH6,0-7,0, and 2:3:4 fertilizer should be used in the basic fertilizer programme.

114

The small 25 g supplementary nitrogen side-dressing should be applied 4-8 weeks after germination.

Succession: Because of the long growing season, successional sowings are not recommended. A late winter–early spring sowing will give a summer crop, but yields and quality will be lower than a winter-grown crop.

Sow: Direct and do not transplant. Germination of parsnip seed is seldom good. Thick sowings are recommended and, if a good stand emerges, thinning should be done as soon as possible.

Seed loses viability rapidly and should not be held over from one season to the next. Germination is slow: soaking seeds in warm water for 24 hours will reduce the germination time. Fluid sowing of pregerminated seeds will cut the emergence period by 7-14 days. Seed count — 200-350 seeds: 1 g.

Spacing guide: Conventional — rows 400-700 mm and 75-150 mm within-row.
High-density — rows 300 mm and 100 mm within-row. For smaller roots, rows 200 mm and 75 mm within-row.

Harvest: Winter-grown parsnips are ready to harvest about 25 weeks from sowing. They may be left in the soil until required, but should be lifted before the end of winter. A summer-grown crop will be ready about five weeks earlier.

Pests and diseases: There are no serious pests and diseases. Larvae of the scarab beetle may attack young roots in summer. Mole-rats are attracted by the sweet roots.

Points to watch: Young plants need plenty of moisture. Watch for signs of mole-rat damage — leaf wilting.

GROWING VEGETABLES

PEA

Region	Jan.	Feb.	Mar.	Apr.	May	Jun.	Jul.	Aug.	Sep.	Oct.	Nov.	Dec.
1												
2					■	■	■	■				
3					■	■	■					
4				■	■	■	■	■				
5				■	■		■	■				
6				■	■	■	■					

Peas are grown in all regions with varying degrees of success. Some of the main problems are frost damage, powdery mildew, poor germination in cold soils, seed rotting in too warm soils and comparatively low yields for the space used, over a long period.

This is a cool season crop and should be grown so that harvesting is completed before the onset of hot weather. Planning can be a critical factor in the success of growing peas. They can stand moderate frost without damage to the vines, but if plants are flowering, flowers and young pods will be killed by a light frost. Severe frost may kill the entire plant.

Soil: Too much organic matter in the soil may encourage excessive vine growth at the expense of pods. Soils should be slightly acid, pH6,0-7,0 but acid soils down to 5,5 are also suitable.

Use either of the blends in the basic fertilizer programme. In slightly acid or neutral soils the supplementary nitrogen side-dressing may be omitted as plants collect nitrogen from the air and 'fix' it so that it may be used by the plants. In more acid soils a single 25 g application should be given when flowering begins.

Succession: Depending on space and climate, successional sowings may be made at 3-4 weekly intervals.

Sow: Direct and do not transplant. Soil temperatures influence germination. Thinning should be done early to avoid root disturbance and excessive competition. Seed count — 300-400 seeds: 100 g.

Spacing guide: Conventional — rows 450 mm-1,0 m depending on the cultivar and 25-75 mm within-row.
High density — three-row broad-band at 100-120 mm square with 450 mm between each broad-band. Single row spacing 200 mm with 50 mm within-row.

Harvest: The period between sowing and harvesting varies between 15 and 25 weeks depending on sowing and time, growing conditions and cultivars. The cropping period is 3-4 weeks but longer for tall-vined cultivars. Regular picking encourages new pod setting.

Pests and diseases: American bollworm, aphids, damping-off, downy mildew, leaf miner, powdery mildew, pre-emergence damping-off, and red spider mite.

Points to watch: Soils should be as weed free as possible and regular weeding is important: peas cannot tolerate competition for moisture and nutrients. Unless powdery mildew resistant cultivars are grown a regular, preventive spraying programme should be used at the first sign of infection.

Support for tall-vined cultivars is essential and some support for shorter ones is recommended. Avoid deep cultivation as roots may be damaged. Pick pods carefully to avoid disturbing roots. Protect with bird netting. Pick pods in the early morning or immediately before freezing.

PEPPER

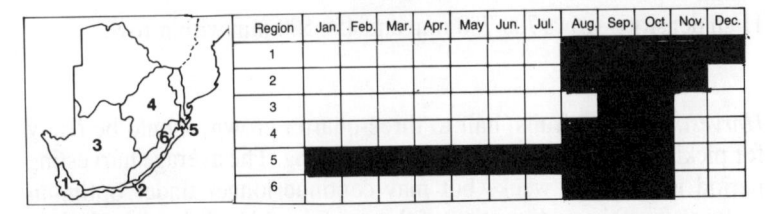

Region	Jan.	Feb.	Mar.	Apr.	May	Jun.	Jul.	Aug.	Sep.	Oct.	Nov.	Dec.
1								■	■	■	■	■
2								■	■		■	■
3								■		■	■	■
4							■	■	■	■	■	■
5	■	■	■	■	■	■	■	■	■	■	■	■
6												

Peppers, also known as capsicums, are classed in two main groups — bell or sweet, and hot or cayenne. Hot peppers contain more of the pungent compound, capsaicin, than sweet peppers. Green peppers normally grown in gardens are immature red or yellow sweet peppers which, when ripe, are sweeter and richer in vitamins A and C.

Bell peppers are usually large and blocky with three or four lobes. Hot peppers are also green when immature, some are sweet and mainly used for canning or processing, while most are hot, usually long, slim and tapered and used for pickling, curry powders and sauces.

Soil: Plants are heavy feeders and have a long growing season requiring a highly soil. The soil pH range is between 5,5 and 6,5. Use 2:3:4 in the basic fertilizer programme.

Split the 50 g supplementary nitrogen side-dressing into two 25 g applications, the first when flowering starts and the second about a month later.

Deep waterings are necessary. In loose soils, such as deep-beds, plants may need supporting as they develop.

Succession: Successional sowings are not necessary.

Sow: In seedtrays, preferably with bottom heat in late winter and early spring. Plants are susceptible to cold and must not receive any growth check. Allow 6-10 weeks to reach transplanting size.

Rapid growth must be maintained throughout the growing season. If peppers and eggplants prematurely flower and set fruits when plants are small, growth and yield will be retarded. Seed count — 100-200 seeds: 1 g.

Spacing guide: Conventional — rows 600-900 mm and 300-600 mm within-row.
High density — rows 700-750 mm and 450-500 mm within-row.

Harvest: The first fruits, half to three-quarter grown, should be ready for picking about 11 weeks from transplanting. The average harvesting period is about 12 weeks but may continue longer under optimum growing conditions. A portion of the stem should be left on the fruits.

Pests and diseases: There are no serious pests and diseases. Aphids, bacterial spot, powdery mildew, red spider mite and thrips may cause occasional damage.

Points to watch: Do not plant in cold soils. Peppers are usually self-regulating when setting fruits. Flowers normally drop off if a plant is yielding to full capacity. Flower setting recommences after some fruits are harvested. Water stress and high temperatures may also cause flower drop.

Support heavily laden branches. Take extra care when transplanting and keep as much soil around roots as possible as root damage seriously delays growth.

THE BASIC VEGETABLES

POTATO

Region	Jan.	Feb.	Mar.	Apr.	May	Jun.	Jul.	Aug.	Sep.	Oct.	Nov.	Dec.
1												
2												
3												
4												
5												
6												

The size of the garden will dictate whether or not potatoes are grown as a summer or autumn crop. They require considerable space as they are usually ridged to prevent near-surface tubers being exposed to light.

Soil: Light soils with plenty of organic matter are preferred. The basic fertilizer programme should be amended. Retain the 200 g superphosphate but double the 2:3:4 rate to 200 g.

Soil pH should be between 5,5 and 6,0. Lime should be applied only if soils are excessively acid.

Two 50 g applications of the supplementary nitrogen side-dressing should be given when the plants are growing vigorously and about four weeks later.

Succession: Successional plantings may be made through the recommended planting period. The potato is basically a cool-season crop and usually gives the best results from an early spring planting.

Plant: Tubers should be planted in trenches 100 mm deep in contact with moist soil and covered with 50-75 mm soil.

Potato seed should be well sprouted before planting. *Left:* not sufficiently sprouted. *Centre:* ideal for planting. *Right:* sprouts are too advanced.

Five to eight weeks after planting, when plants are 300-500 mm high and standing upright, soil should be ridged up against the plants. Further ridging is usually necessary to protect near-surface tubers. Rapid growth must be maintained.

GROWING VEGETABLES

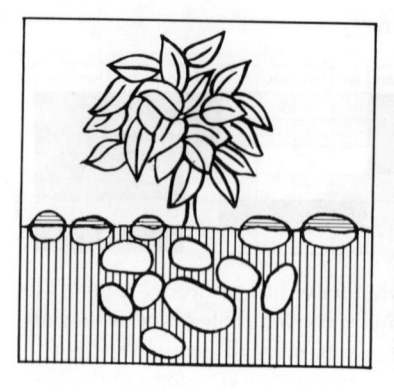

Potato ridging starts 5-8 weeks after planting. Further ridging may be necessary to protect near-surface tubers.

Spacing guide: Conventional — rows 600-900 mm and 300-450 mm within-row.
High-density — rows 750 mm, and 250 mm within-row.

Harvest: After 16-20 weeks foliage dies off and growth ceases. During the next three to four weeks the skins suberise (harden) and are then fully mature. If potatoes are not needed for storage, harvesting may begin several weeks earlier when tubers are smaller and used as fresh 'new' potatoes.

Pests and diseases: Main ones are the virus disease leaf roll, mosaic viruses, bacterial wilt, early and late blight, powdery mildew, fusarium wilt, aphids, cutworms, millipedes, potato tuber moth, black maize beetle and common scab.

Points to watch: Some cultivars are better adapted to certain areas than others, while some are more suitable for spring planting than summer. There are cultivars with more disease resistance than others. Some cultivars have been bred for processing and are not particularly suitable as table potatoes.

   Local advice should be obtained before choosing a cultivar. Use certified seed. Tubers exposed to sun turn green and then contain a toxic element: they must not be eaten.

RADISH

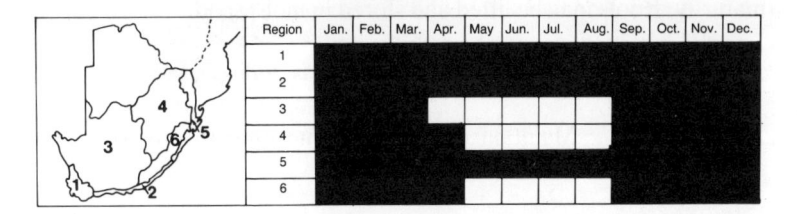

Region	Jan.	Feb.	Mar.	Apr.	May	Jun.	Jul.	Aug.	Sep.	Oct.	Nov.	Dec.
1												
2												
3												
4												
5												
6												

There are two types of radish grown in vegetable gardens, summer and winter radish. Summer radish can be grown from spring to autumn and mature quickly, within four weeks under good growing conditions. Winter radish are autumn sown and take longer to mature.

Soil: Soil pH should be between 6,0 and 7,0. Either of the blends may be used in the basic fertilizer programme. The supplementary nitrogen side-dressing should not be necessary for summer radish. If growth is slow, a single 25 g application may be given.

A single 25 g side-dressing should be given to winter radish 4-6 weeks after sowing.

Succession: Sowings may be made every 7-14 days or as required from spring to autumn. Under hot conditions radish mature rapidly and become pithy, pungent and coarse if left in the soil too long.

A mixture of cultivars sown together may extend the cropping period by a few days.

Sow: Direct and do not transplant. Seed count — 70-150 seeds: 1 g.

Spacing guide: Conventional — rows 200-500 mm and 15-30 mm within-row for summer radish. The larger-rooted winter radish row spacing is 450-650 mm and 100-200 mm within-row.
High density — summer radish: broad band 20-25 mm square. Double rows 100-150 mm and 20-25 mm within-row, with 250 mm between each set of double rows.

Harvest: Roots are ready for harvesting as soon as they are large enough. Round cultivars may be pulled when marble size. They should be used before reaching full maturity, while still crisp. Most summer radish are ready 20-30 days from sowing under optimum conditions, but take one or two weeks longer in cool weather. Variation in maturity of summer cultivars can be 7-10 days.

Winter radish, Black Spanish type, take up to eight weeks to reach maturity. Roots may be lifted and stored in moist sand.

Pests and diseases: There are no serious pests or diseases.

Points to watch: Maintain constant soil moisture to promote rapid growth. Avoid overcrowding.

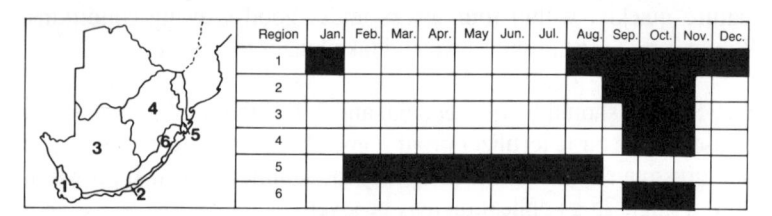

SQUASH

Region	Jan.	Feb.	Mar.	Apr.	May	Jun.	Jul.	Aug.	Sep.	Oct.	Nov.	Dec.
1	■								■	■	■	
2									■	■	■	
3										■	■	
4										■	■	
5	■	■	■	■	■	■	■				■	■
6										■	■	

The squash family is rather confusing because it includes several species. The main ones grown in Southern Africa are winter squash, summer squash and pumpkins. Within each group there are various classes and cultivars differing in appearance, flavour, colour, shape, size and vine characteristics.

Squash and pumpkins generally require a lot of space — even bush cultivars need more space than most other vegetables — and space requirements have to be considered in limited-area gardens as few of the trailing cultivars can be successfully trained up supports.

They are easy to grow and, being of tropical or subtropical origin, thrive in hot, humid conditions and warm nights. Under ideal temperatures plants grow rapidly and some summer squash produce edible fruits within six or seven weeks from sowing.

Soil: Squash and pumpkins are not exacting in their soil requirements, but tend to be sensitive to too acid or too alkaline soils, preferring a pH range between 6,5 and 7,5.

They respond to liberal amounts of organic matter, preferably well-rotted manure or compost.

Either blend may be used in the basic fertilizer programme. The supplementary nitrogen side-dressing is split into two 25 g applications, the first when flowering begins and then 3-4 weeks later.

Squash and pumpkins have large, deep root systems in addition to a near-surface network. In deep soils roots can penetrate to depths of 1 m or more. The huge leaves give off moisture into the air (transpiration) necessary for cooling and, combined with the large root system, plants require copious amounts of water.

Ground watering is recommended as moisture on leaves may encourage foliar diseases. It is normal for leaves to droop slightly on hot days, but they pick up again in the late afternoon or evening. If not, soak the soil.

Succession: Two sowings of summer squash — those harvested at an immature stage — at 1-2 month intervals within the recommended sowing period will extend the cropping season. Successional sowings of winter — storage — squash and pumpkins are not normally made.

Sow: Direct and do not transplant unless starting in a deep planting bag. Seedlings must not receive any growth check.

Seed may be soaked in warm water for 24 hours to speed germination and soften 'hard' seeds resistant to water uptake. Longer soaking should be avoided.

Sow two or three seeds to a hill (bowl) and thin to the strongest growing one as soon as possible. Seed count — 40-110 seeds: 10 g.

Spacing guide: Conventional — bush: rows 900 mm-1,5 m and 450 mm-1,2 m within-row.
Recommended — rows 900 mm and 600-750 mm within-row.
Trailing (vining) — depending on the vigour of the cultivar, rows 900 mm-3,0 m and 900 mm-2,5 m within-row.
Recommended — rows 1,8-2,5 m and 900 mm-1,0 m within-row. Pumpkins need a similar spacing to trailing squash.

Harvest: Courgette squash produce edible fruits quickly and continue for 4-10 weeks if regularly harvested. Other summer squash may be harvested 8-12 weeks from sowing. Regular picking will also encourage new fruits to form. The cropping period varies according to the cultivar.

Harvesting of winter squash and pumpkins is done only when fruits are fully mature. Some may mature after 12-15 weeks from sowing, while late-maturing ones will be ready to harvest only after 15-20 weeks.

Pests and diseasesa: Main pests and diseases are aphids, powdery mildew and fruit (pumpkin) flies. Virus and wilt diseases cannot be controlled.

Points to watch: Regular picking of summer squash. Avoid sowing in too cold soil, watch for powdery mildew, particularly in later sowings. Avoid deep cultivation because of near-surface roots.

Thinning plants to three or four fruits will give larger winter squash or pumpkins but will also decrease total yield. Maintain fertility and moisture at optimum levels to reduce any stress that may cause plants to abort young fruits.

SWEET-CORN

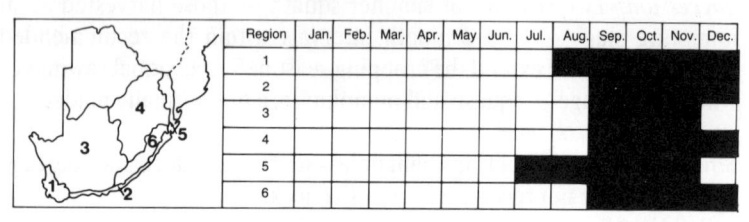

Region	Jan.	Feb.	Mar.	Apr.	May	Jun.	Jul.	Aug.	Sep.	Oct.	Nov.	Dec.
1												
2												
3												
4												
5												
6												

Sweet-corn is an easy and interesting vegetable to grow but one that must be used as soon as harvested to be fully appreciated. Cobs purchased in shops have invariably lost much of their sugar content and often are not much sweeter than ordinary maize.

It has become more popular since the introduction of F_1 hybrids, because overall yields are higher, quality and flavour are better, cobs are sweeter and often more sugar retentive.

Soil: A moderately acid soil between pH5,5 and 6,5 is required for optimum growth. Use 2:3:4 in the basic fertilizer programme. Nutrient-deficient plants will be stunted and never recover to produce satisfactory cobs.

The supplementary nitrogen side-dressing, in two 25 g applications, should be given when plants are 200-300 mm high and again at 500 mm.

Sweet-corn needs a continuous and adequate moisture supply throughout the growing period. Critical times are when the plants are young and need to grow rapidly and from tasseling time through to harvest. If plants are checked through lack of water, yields will be lower.

Tasseling time is when the male flower spike is open and pollen is free. The silk is an elongated stigma appearing at the top of the developing cob.

In hot weather plants may transpire water faster than roots absorb it, but if there is adequate soil moisture wilting, in the form of leaf rolling, will be temporary.

Succession: Several block sowings during the recommended sowing season at 2-3 weekly intervals will provide sweet-corn over several weeks. The main limitation for successional sowings is space.

Sow: Direct and do not transplant. Sow in small blocks of 3-4 rows and not in long single rows as sweet-corn is wind pollinated. Seed count — 40-80 seeds: 10 g.

Spacing guide: Conventional — 750 mm-1,0 m and 250-450 mm within-row.
Recommended — rows 900 mm and 300 mm within-row or 600 by 400 mm. Too-close spacing reduces yields.

Harvest: Cobs are ready for picking 11-12 weeks from germination, depending on growing conditions and cultivars. The period is shortened from a midsummer sowing. There is no extended cropping season as cobs should be picked at the 'milk' stage.

Pests and diseases: Black maize beetle, chafer beetle, stalk borer.

Points to watch: Do not sow in cold soils. Grow F_1 hybrid cultivars.

SWISS CHARD

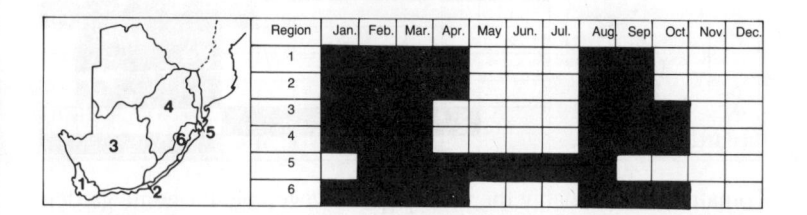

Swiss chard is a year-round substitute for spinach as it withstands heat and frost. It is a type of beet grown for its large, crisp leaves and fleshy stalks. Roots are not eaten.

It is easy to grow and needs little attention when established.

Soil: Plants have a long growing season so that soils should be high in fertility with a pH 6,0-7,0 range. Either of the two fertilizers may be used in the basic fertilizer programme.

Two 50 g applications of the supplementary side-dressing should be given a month after germination and 4-5 weeks later.

GROWING VEGETABLES

Succession: A spring, midsummer and autumn sowing should ensure year-round cropping.

Sow: Direct or transplant. Allow 4-6 weeks to reach transplanting size. Seed count 400-550 seeds: 10 g.

Spacing guide: Conventional — rows 600-900 mm and 200-400 mm within-row.
Recommended — rows 600 mm and 200-250 mm within-row.

Harvest: The first picking may be made 8-10 weeks from sowing or 6-8 weeks from transplanting. The cropping period is 3-4 months or longer.

Pests and diseases: There are no serious pests or diseases. Leaf spot, if allowed to develop, will reduce the number of harvestable leaves.

Points to watch: Maintain rapid growth. Harvest outer leaves first. If leaves are damaged or diseased, cut back the entire plant to 25-50 mm above the crown and new leaves will be produced if plants are not too old.

TOMATO

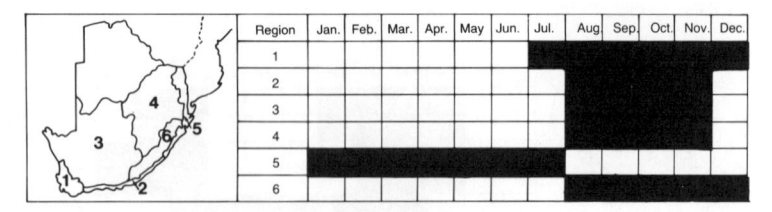

Region	Jan.	Feb.	Mar.	Apr.	May	Jun.	Jul.	Aug.	Sep.	Oct.	Nov.	Dec.
1							■	■	■	■	■	
2							■	■	■	■	■	
3							■	■	■	■		
4						■	■	■	■	■	■	
5	■	■	■	■	■	■	■					
6							■	■	■			

Tomatoes are probably the most popular vegetable for home gardens because they are not too difficult to grow if given reasonable attention, they have a distinctive flavour, are versatile in the many ways they can be used — and about 10 well-grown plants can supply an average family's requirements for most of the summer.

For optimum use of space indeterminate cultivars will continue to grow and produce fruits over a long period. Determinate ones produce their crop over a shorter period, have a more compact growth habit and are more suitable for container growing.

A careful choice of cultivars also helps in successful tomato growing. In addition to high-yielding F_1 hybrids, there are also cultivars with resistance to several serious diseases and nematodes.

THE BASIC VEGETABLES

Tomatoes grown in cages can produce very high yields. The wire mesh should be wide enough to put a hand through to pick the lower fruits and strong enough to support the heavy plants.

Soil: Tomatoes grow well in most soils. Fertility must be high as plants are heavy feeders, have extensive root systems and a long growing season, particularly in the case of indeterminate cultivars.

Soil pH should be between 5,5 and 6,5. In strongly acid soils lime should be added several weeks before bed preparation.

In the basic fertilizer programme 2:3:4 is preferred to 2:3:2. The split 50 g supplementary nitrogen side-dressing should be given when the first fruits set with the second 25 g about a month later. A further 25 g application may be given later if the plants need a boost.

Deep waterings are essential as root systems spread and in deep soils penetrate to a metre or more.

Succession: Small monthly sowings to supply 2-4 plants or larger sowings at the beginning of the main sowing period, followed by another sowing 2-3 months later, will give an extended cropping season. A similar programme may be used in region 5 during the January–July period.

Sow: In seedtrays, preferably with bottom heat in late winter and early spring. Seedlings are susceptible to cold and must not suffer any growth check. The period between sowing and transplanting will be 5-7 weeks, but possibly a week or two longer in cool conditions.

Repeated transplanting of tomatoes usually results in higher yields. Seeds sown in seedtrays should be transplanted when they are in the seedleaf stage — before true leaves form — as deeply as possible into small pots. As the plants develop to 4-6 sets of leaves they are again transplanted, deeper than before, into slightly larger pots or planting bags. Leaves should be removed if lower than the new planting depth.

As soon as the plants are again growing well they are ready for final transplanting, leaving only six sets of leaves above soil level. This method of deep planting is applicable only to tomatoes.

During the repeated potting on plants should be gradually hardened off so that they receive a minimum set-back when planted out into the garden or containers. Seed count — 250-350 seeds: 1 g.

Spacing guide: Conventional — unpruned: rows 900 mm-1,5 m and 600-900 mm within-row. Pruned: rows 900 mm-1,2 m and 300-600 mm within-row.

High dennsity — single stem: rows 750 mm and 300-450 mm within-row. Multiple stem, pruned: rows 900 mm-1 m and 500 mm within-row. Determinate and bush types 500 mm square.

Harvest: Depending on growing conditions and cultivars, harvesting commences 9-13 weeks from transplanting. Indeterminate cultivars can produce fruits for 12 weeks or longer if well grown and not damaged by pests or diseases. Determinate cultivars vary in the cropping period depending on when plant growth terminates.

Pests and diseases: Main pests and diseases are: American bollworm, bacterial spot, early and late blight, plusia looper, powdery mildew, red spider mite, rust mite and thrips. A number of bacterial, wilt and virus diseases may also attack tomatoes but are not usually controllable when once established.

Points to watch: Do not let plants grow too large before transplanting. Maintain a regular pest and disease control programme. Avoid excessive shade and do not plant in cold soils.

Avoid too much or too little water, do not overfertilize, particularly nitrogen. If plants are to be pruned and staked, put the stakes into the soil before planting to avoid damage to roots. Single-stem pruning gives larger fruits but a lower overall yield than unpruned or pruned multi-stem plants.

Do not let fruits lie on the soil. Avoid splashing foliage when watering. Use cultivars resistant to some of the serious diseases and pests, such as verticillium and fusarium wilts, nematodes and tobacco mosaic. Disease resistance is usually shown with capital letters after the cultivar name. For example, a cultivar resistant to the two wilt diseases and nematodes will have the letters VFN.

TURNIP

Region	Jan.	Feb.	Mar.	Apr.	May	Jun.	Jul.	Aug.	Sep.	Oct.	Nov.	Dec.
1												
2												
3												
4												
5												
6												

Turnips are a cool-weather crop but may be grown in late winter or early spring before there is too much heat.

Soil: The soil pH range is between 5,5 and 7,0. The 2:3:4 blend should be used in the basic fertilizer programme and a single supplementary nitrogen side-dressing should be given when roots show signs of swelling.

Succession: Successional sowings may be made as required for autumn and winter harvesting, but in most regions spring sowings should be limited to late July, August and early September.

Sow: Direct and do not transplant. Seed count — 300-500 seeds: 1 g.

Spacing guide: Conventional — rows 300-750 mm and 50-100 mm within-row.
High density — rows 300-350 mm and 25-50 mm within-row.

Harvest: 6-11 weeks from sowing, depending on the cultivar and season. Turnips should be harvested before reaching maturity. Under cool, winter conditions they may be left in the soil after reaching full size for a few weeks if necessary.

Pests and diseases: There are no serious pests and diseases. Small beetles and grasshoppers may chew young seedlings.

Points to watch: In warm weather roots rapidly become bitter, pithy and strongly flavoured if grown to full size. Quality and yield will be reduced if plants are subjected to water stress. In adverse spring growing conditions plants may bolt before forming roots.

WATERMELON

Region	Jan.	Feb.	Mar.	Apr.	May	Jun.	Jul.	Aug.	Sep.	Oct.	Nov.	Dec.
1									■	■	■	■
2									■	■	■	
3									■		■	■
4									■	■		
5							■	■	■			
6								■	■			

Watermelons are grown in the same way as muskmelon but usually require more space. Some cultivars have semi-compact, relatively short-branched vines suitable for larger vegetable gardens. Fruits vary in size, shape, colour, flesh colour and maturity times.

Soil: Plants require soils with high fertility and organic matter, preferably well-rotted manure. The hill system enables manure to be placed in concentrated form under where the plants grow. The pH range is between 5,0 and 7,0.

Use 2:3:2 in the basic fertilizer programme and split the supplementary nitrogen side-dressing into two 25 g applications, the first when fruits begin to form and again 3-4 weeks later.

Succession: Space permitting, two or more sowings may be made within the recommended sowing period.

Sow: Direct. If seeds are sown in small planting bags, they must not receive any root check. Sow two or three seeds in a hill and thin to the strongest growing one as early as possible. Seed count — 5-15 seeds: 1 g.

Spacing guide: Conventional — rows 1,8-2,5 m and 900 mm-2 m within-row. Hills should be spaced about 2 m apart each way. If two plants are to be grown to each hill, increase spacing to 2,5-3,0 m.

Harvest: Fruits should ripen on the vines 9-14 weeks from sowing, depending on the cultivar. Fruits must be fully ripe when harvested.

Pests and diseases: Anthracnose, aphids, downy mildew, fruit (pumpkin) flies, red spider mite and thrips.

Points to watch: Older cultivars may produce only one or two fruits a plant. Newer F_1 cultivars should give higher yields. As it is large-fruited with a large leaf area, copious amounts of water are needed throughout the growing season.

11
Lesser grown and known vegetables

Vegetables discussed in this chapter will give both experienced gardeners and newcomers to vegetable gardening an introduction to some of the lesser grown and known ones.

Once the growing of basic vegetables becomes a matter of course, keen vegetable gardeners want to extend their experience and enjoy vegetables that are not often otherwise available. Growing some of these less common vegetables provides a stimulating challenge.

Basic Fertilizer Programme:
The programme discussed in the introduction to Basic Vegetables, may be used and adapted each spring for perennial vegetables. Use 2:3:2 for: Chinese cabbage, endive, okra, rhubarb and spinach.
Use 2:3:4 for: Globe and Jerusalem artichokes, asparagus, celery, celeriac, chicory, garlic, horseradish, kohlrabi, salsify, swede and sweet potato.
Use either for: Florence fennel, kale, onion types.

Supplementary nitrogen side-dressing:
Where applicable the single or split applications are referred to under the heading SNS (supplementary nitrogen side-dressing).

ARTICHOKE, GLOBE. The edible portions are the thickened bases of the bracts and the soft fleshy part at the base of the immature flower head.

The plant is perennial and needs a soil with high organic matter content. A long, cool growing season is preferred otherwise buds open rapidly and bracts become tough and fibrous.

The best method of propagation is to take rooted suckers or sprouts from the base of plants in early winter or spring. Propagation from seed may result in variable types and germination is often poor. Plant 1,5-2 m apart.

SNS: Three 50 g applications scattered around each plant in early spring, when buds appear and after harvest.

Buds are usually cooked, after which the hairy centre or 'choke' is removed and filled with a cheese or hollandaise sauce. The heart at the base of the bud is a delicacy.

ARTICHOKE, JERUSALEM. A perennial member of the sunflower family, grown for its edible tubers. Tubers are usually lifted in winter and planted in spring.

Plants grow in a wide range of soils, from poor to fertile, prefer a cool growing season, but tolerate heat. Whole or tuber pieces are planted 100 mm deep, 350-600 mm within-row, depending on soil fertility, and row spacing 750 mm-1 m.

SNS: Two 25 g applications when plants are growing vigorously and at flowering time.

Tubers do not store as well as potatoes because of their thin skins and are often left in the soil until needed. They should be lifted before new growth starts otherwise they may become invasive.

Main uses are as a cooked vegetable with sauce or as a soup.

ASPARAGUS. A perennial vegetable, grown for its soft edible spears. Plants grow well in most well-drained soils of medium to good fertility.

One-year-old crowns should be planted in preference to starting from seed. Spacing between beds (rows) should be 1,2-1,5 m, 450 mm within-row and 200-250 mm deep, initially covered with only 50 mm soil. As shoots develop the trench should be gradually filled.

Plants should not suffer water stress during active growth. For the first two full growing seasons harvesting should be avoided to enable plants to build up extensive root systems. During this period the fern-like foliage developing from the spears should be allowed to grow and die back before being removed.

Harvesting should be restricted to 2-3 weeks in the third season, gradually increasing to eight weeks in the fifth season and thereafter. Ridging during harvest will increase spear size, but ridges should be levelled when harvesting has been completed. Female plants, identified by berries later in the season, yield less than male plants.

Use 2:3:4 as a side-dressing at 125 g a running metre before growth starts and repeat when harvesting has finished to promote fern growth.

SNS: Two 25 g applications when the first spears appear and again 2-3 weeks later.

Asparagus spears are cooked and eaten with melted butter, or used cold in salads and in savoury tarts.

CABBAGE, CHINESE. A versatile vegetable used like lettuce, cooked like cabbage, shredded for coleslaw, baked in a light savoury custard or used in soups. The flavour is a cross between cabbage, lettuce and celery.

Sow direct in rows 450-600 mm and thin to 200-300 mm within-row. Allow 12 weeks plus from sowing to harvest.

SNS: Two 25 g applications four weeks after germination and again 3-4 weeks later.

Grow as an autumn to early winter crop as plants bolt in hot weather.

CELERY. There are two main types, green and self-blanching. The latter is normally grown in trenches and ridged to blanch the leaf stems. Green celery is not ridged.

This is not an easy vegetable to grow successfully as it requires continuous soil moisture and high fertility. Seed is also difficult to germinate. Buying established plants from a nursery is recommended.

Adjust the basic fertilizer programme to 150 g 2:3:4 and dig in together with organic matter, fairly shallowly as plants do not have deep root systems.

SNS: Two 50 g applications 3-6 weeks after transplanting and again 4-6 weeks later.

Trenched celery — 250 mm deep, 750-900 mm rows and 200-250 mm within-row. Green celery — reduce row spacing to 600 mm. Self-blanching celery — 300 by 250 mm or 250-280 mm square. Allow 15-20 weeks from transplanting.

Leaves may be used for stocks, hearts can be braised with a cheese sauce, stems are used in fresh salads and stems and leaves are used in soups.

CELERIAC. Closely related to celery but grown for its thickened stem-root 'bulbs'.

Cultivation is similar to celery. Plant 150-200 mm apart (rows 700-750 mm) or 400 mm square for larger roots. Celeriac may be harvested when 50-100 mm in diameter. Allow 15-20 weeks from transplanting. Commercially grown transplants are rare.

May be used in the same way as potatoes, but takes longer to cook, grated as a salad topping, sliced and boiled and served with a French dressing as an hors d'oeuvre, thinly sliced in fresh salads and for soups.

CHICORY, WITLOOF. Grown for winter forcing to produce blanched chicons (shoots or heads).

Sow direct in spring — too early sowing may result in bolting. Thin to 100-150 mm within-row with 400-450 mm rows. Allow 15-18 weeks for mature roots from sowing.
SNS: 25 g 4-8 weeks after germination.

Roots may be lifted in late autumn or left in the soil. Leaves are trimmed back to within 50 mm of the crown. Lifted roots are planted 100-150 mm deep with the crown at soil level, then covered with 150-200 mm sawdust, sand, peat, vermiculite or other porous material. In-ground roots also need a similar ridge cover. In 2-4 weeks blanched, tightly folded heads (chicons) will be ready for harvesting.

Mainly used as a fresh salad vegetable with or without a dressing. Whole heads may be cooked with various seasonings.

ENDIVE. There are two main types of endive: curled with loose, narrow, pale to medium-green, finely cut, fringed leaves which blanch to form a creamy white centre; and Batavian with large, broad, slightly twisted, lettuce-like leaves forming a loose head with partial blanching of the inner foliage.

If heads are loosely tied to encourage blanching, bitterness is reduced. Bitterness is more pronounced in hot weather. Outer leaves should be discarded.

Grow as lettuce throughout the year. In cold soils plants may bolt. Sow direct or transplant, but do not transplant in hot weather. Rows 450-600 mm and 250-300 mm within-row. Allow 12-14 weeks for harvestable heads. Leaf picking can start earlier.
SNS: Two 25 g applications, six weeks after sowing and four weeks later.

Use as a lettuce substitute.

FLORENCE FENNEL. Not to be confused with the Fennel herb. Florence Fennel is a variety of the herb, producing a bulbous stem with a slight aniseed flavour.

Sow direct in spring or in summer for an early winter crop. Thin plants to 450 mm square. Ridge soil, 3-4 weeks before harvest to blanch stems. Allow at least 20 weeks from sowing to harvest.
SNS: Two 25 g applications, a month after germination and 4-6 weeks later.

Used fresh in salads with French dressing. It may also be cooked and served in a cheese sauce. May be used with a wide range of chicken, fish and meat dishes.

GARLIC. There are two types grown in Southern Africa, a large, white type and a pink one. The latter has a better quality and longer storage life.

Plant between April and May in rows 400-600 mm apart and 50-100 mm within-row. Allow 25-30 weeks to mature when foliage dries and topples. Increase the 2:3:4 fertilizer from 100 g/m^2 to 150 g.

SNS: Two 25 g applications 5-7 weeks after planting and again 4-6 weeks later.

Cloves may be stored dry or peeled and covered in cooking oil.

HORSERADISH. A hardy perennial grown for its pungent roots which are grated and used in various sauces or on its own mixed with cream and vinegar.

It is grown from root-cuttings or 'sets'. Soil must be deep and fertile.

Plant 200-300 mm long root-cuttings, taken from lateral roots or lower parts of the main root in autumn or spring. Plant vertically or on a slant 50-100 mm deep with 600-750 mm between plants. Do not plant upside down.

Under good growing conditions, harvestable roots may be obtained in autumn from a spring planting. Roots may be lifted as required thereafter. It may become invasive unless controlled.

SNS: A single 25 g application when plants are growing well.

KALE: Also known as borecole or curly kale. Leaves may be used as a substitute for spinach or cabbage. Young leaves may be used in salads.

Sow direct or transplant, 450 mm square between January and March.

SNS: Two 50 g applications 4-6 weeks from transplanting, or 8-10 weeks from germination and again when the first leaves are harvested. Allow 8-12 weeks from transplanting. The harvesting period can last for eight weeks or longer.

It has a strong flavour and takes longer to cook than most green vegetables. Often served with seasoning and vinegar.

KOHLRABI. The edible portion is a large 'bulb' produced on a stem above ground, rather resembling a turnip but with leaves sprouting out of it.

Sow direct in late summer, autumn, late winter and early spring in

most regions and between February and June in region 5. Rows 300-500 mm and 100-150 mm within-row. Allow 8-10 weeks from sowing to harvest.
SNS: A single 25 g application when roots begin to swell.

Kohlrabi is an excellent autumn and winter vegetable. It may be eaten raw or cooked and has a mild, sweet turnip flavour.

Kohlrabi may be eaten raw or cooked. It has a mild, sweet turnip flavour.

MUSTARD SPINACH. Also called mustard greens. Plants have large, broad, thick, dark-green leaves with a flavour combining mustard and spinach. Cooked like cabbage leaves.
Plants mature in 5-6 weeks and, although tolerant of heat, should be sown during cooler periods for better plants and superior flavour.
Sow direct in 300-400 mm rows and thin to 100-200 mm within-row. If soil is reasonably fertile, the basic fertilizer programme is not necessary.

OKRA. Immature seed pods are the edible part of okra. Plants are fairly large and occupy space from spring to late summer.
Soak seeds overnight for better and faster germination. Sow direct in rows 900 mm-1,2 m and thin plants to 400-500 mm within-row. Do not sow in cold soils.

Allow 8-10 weeks from sowing to the first picking. Harvest every 2-3 days, using a sharp knife, when pods are 100-120 mm long, before they become fibrous.

SNS: Two 25 g applications when the first pods have set and 4-6 weeks later. Excessive nitrogen reduces pod setting.

Pods add body and flavour to soups, stews and relishes and may be cooked or mixed with tomatoes or deep-fried in egg and crumbs.

ONION TYPES. Chives are perennial and have a mild onion flavour. Propagate by seed or division. Frequent cutting encourages new growth. Flowers should be removed as they appear otherwise the plant becomes semi-dormant. Space 200-250 mm apart each way.

Salad, green or spring onions are harvested when young. Non-bulbing cultivars are preferred. Sow thickly in rows or bands from spring to early winter.

Shallots are the finest flavoured of all onions. Mainly grown for dry bulbs but also used as salad onions when young. The shallot is a clump of small bulbs rather similar to garlic.

Cultural methods are similar to garlic, but allow a few weeks longer to mature and use a 150 mm within-row spacing.

Pickling onions are usually sown in spring in poor soil to encourage fast and small bulbing. Seed should be sown thickly in a broad-band. No manure, compost or fertilizer is used.

Other onion types include a perennial multiplier called the Egyptian or tree onion, which produces clusters of bulblets at the top of stems.

The Japanese onion is a bunching multiplier, which can be divided and replanted throughout the year.

With the exception of pickling onions, use the garlic fertilizer programme.

RHUBARB. Propagation is by division of crowns in spring. Each part of the crown must have roots and at least one bud. Do not crop in the first year, thereafter gradually increase as plants become well established.

Add liberal quantities of manure or compost before planting and space 900 mm-1,2 m apart each way. Renew manure at the end of each winter.

SNS: Two 25 g applications before new leaves appear and after harvesting has finished.

Used in pies, sauces, preserves, or stewed and for home wine-making.

SALSIFY. Also called the oyster plant or vegetable oyster because of its faint oyster-like flavour. The plant is grown for its long, pale-yellow roots and creamy white flesh.

Sow direct in spring in a deeply cultivated, fertile soil. Thin to 75-100 mm within-row (rows 400-450 mm). Allow 15-20 weeks to reach maturity. Roots may be overwintered in the soil if not immediately needed

SNS: A single 25 g side-dressing 8-10 weeks after germination.

May be eaten raw, cooked and served with a cream sauce. Also served with fish and meat dishes, usually parboiled, then fried in butter.

SPINACH. Usually grown only in cool weather as it bolts rapidly in heat.

Sow direct in rows 400-500 mm and thin to 100 mm within-row. Plants are shallow rooted. Allow 7-10 weeks to harvest.

SNS: Two 50 g applications when plants are growing vigorously, 3-4 weeks after emergence, and when harvesting commences. Pick a few leaves at a time to encourage new leaf growth.

Spinach may be cooked, mixed in fresh salads and used with raw mushrooms and bacon bits or as egg Florentine.

SWEDE. A yellow-fleshed, turnip-like vegetable with a rather strong flavour. Slower growing than turnips but less likely to become pithy after reaching maturity.

Sow direct in rows 450-550 mm and thin to 150-200 mm within-row. Sow only in late summer and autumn.

SNS: A single 25 g application when roots begin to swell.

Usually cooked and mashed with pepper, salt, butter, milk and nutmeg.

SWEET POTATO. The sweet potato is a tropical crop and needs about 20 weeks of warm weather to produce good-sized roots. Soil should be light, reasonably fertile and well drained.

Sweet potatoes are grown from 'slips' — rooted cuttings — and planted in rows 1 m apart and 300-400 mm within-row. They may also be planted on 200 mm high ridges and 50-75 mm deep. Planting should not be done until all danger of frost is past and soils are warm.

SNS: Two 25 g applications when plants are growing vigorously and then 4-6 weeks later.

Roots may be roasted, deep-fried, used in stews and in various other ways.

WATERCRESS. This may be grown in cooler parts of the year if there is adequate moisture. In hot weather plants are often attacked by numerous pests. Container growing near a water supply is recommended.

Watercress is grown from cuttings — rooted or otherwise — and seed. Seed should be started in trays and transplanted when about 50 mm high. At all times the soil or growing medium must be constantly moist.

When plants are 150 mm high the growing point should be removed to encourage lateral growth. Space 250-300 mm square. Allow 10 weeks to commencement of picking from sowing and less from cuttings.

Liquid feed with a nitrogenous fertilizer every 3-4 weeks to maintain vigorous growth.

Watercress may be used as a salad vegetable, as a garnish on grilled meat or fish, as a sandwich filling and a soup flavouring. It has an attractive pungent flavour.

12
Pests and Diseases

Pests and diseases are one of the hazards of vegetable gardening, but the degree to which they influence the success or otherwise is usually in the hands of the gardener.

In vegetable gardens pest and disease control is a balance between keeping them under control, as far as possible, and accepting the loss of a few plants, leaves, fruits, roots, pods and malformations as inevitable.

The long-term trend is towards **natural and biological ways of countering pests and diseases**. For example, there are cultivars of various vegetables specifically bred for inbuilt disease and pest resistance.

Many pests and diseases are selective, that is, they will attack only certain types of plants and they are not usually a problem throughout the growing season. They probably appear at a certain stage of a plant's growth or when climatic conditions favour their spread and development.

When growing vegetables there are a few questions to answer: What vegetables are being grown? What pests and diseases are likely to attack them? Which of them cause serious problems? Are there measures to control them? Are these measures available to home gardeners?

All vegetables, to some degree or other, are subjected to pest and disease attacks. It is important to identify, as far as possible, what is attacking and then use the correct control measure.

Keep records of pest and disease problems each season so that when the next season's plantings are made preventive measures can be taken. A pest and disease management programme can make a lot of difference to the success of vegetable gardening.

One of the best ways of reducing the need for chemical controls is good cultural practices, maintaining high fertility and vigorous growth.

Safe use of pesticides
The first rule of safety is to read the precautions and directions on the container's label or leaflet and adhere strictly to them.

Approval labels on pesticide containers state clearly what the product is, what it can be used for, how it is to be used, what its dangers are and what safety precautions must be observed in using it.

Before buying a pesticide, check the label and make sure it lists the name of the pest or disease to be controlled. Use the correct products according to the recommendations, and do not use stronger concentrations or larger dosages than recommended.

Use efficient spraying or dusting apparatus in good working order and free of defects. Never try to clear blocked nozzles by blowing through them by mouth, or siphon a pesticide from a container.

Do not apply pesticides at times when bees and other pollinating insects are active.

Dilute or mix sprays outdoors and keep people and animals away from areas where mixing or spraying is taking place.

Store all pesticides out of reach of children and animals, under lock and key and away from food. Always store pesticides in clearly labelled, closed original containers and destroy empty ones.

COMMON PESTS AND DISEASES OF VEGETABLES

Withholding (safe) period: The numbers shown in brackets after the names of pesticides or vegetables indicate the number of days which should be allowed to elapse between the last application of pesticide and harvesting.

Formulation abbreviations: aes – aerosol; b – bait; dp – dusting powder; ec – emulsifiable concentrate; gran – granular; wp – wettable powder; wsp – water soluble powder.
See pages 148-9 for trade names of active ingredients.

Alternaria (blotch): Mainly attacks carrot, parsley and onion. Leaves become spotted, turn yellow and in severe cases it kills off all foliage. No registered control for home garden use, although a copper spray may prove effective.

American bollworm: Attacks beans, brassicas, peas, potatoes and tomatoes. Larvae may be black, brown, green or pink with an off-white stripe along the sides and abdomen. Causes damage to leaves, flowers, pods and fruit.
Control: chlorpyrifos ec — tomato (4)

Anthracnose: This disease may be a problem on beans and watermelon. Bean pods may have sunken brown spots on pods with black or orange edges and angular spots on leaves. Black specks appear on older watermelon leaves and spread throughout the plant.
Control: mancozeb wp (3).

Aphids: Mainly green or black with a soft, pear-shaped body, usually seen in colonies sucking sap from tender growth of a wide range of vegetables.
Control: carbaryl/gamma-BHC dp — general use (30). Do not use on cucurbits or on cabbages after heads have formed or on tomatoes after fruit has set; chlorpyrifos ec — cabbage and Brussels sprouts (7); deltamethrin/piperonyl butoxide aes — general use (14); D-phenothrin/tetramethrin aes — general use (14); diazinon ec — bean, brassicas, tomato (14); dimethoate wp, ec — bean, cabbage, cauliflower, cucurbits (14); fenthion ec — cucurbits (10); formothion ec — potato (14); gamma-BHC ec — brassicas, bean (not after heads or pods have formed); gamma-BHC dp — bean (30); mercaptothion wp, ec, dp — bean (7), cucurbits (1), tomato (1); mercaptothion/copper oxychloride/sulphur dp — general use (14); mercaptothion/mancozeb/sulphur dp — general use (14); oxydemeton-methyl ec — bean (10), cucurbits (21), cabbage, cauliflower (10), Brussels sprouts (14); pirimicarb aes — cabbage (not after heads have formed); thiometon ec — bean (28), cabbage (28), tomato (7), potato (14).

Astylus beetle: A medium-sized beetle with a black spot on a yellow back. Feeds on flower pollen.
Control: carbaryl dp — general use (14); carbaryl/gamma-BHC dp — general use (30); deltamethrin/piperonyl butoxide aes — general use (14); gamma-BHC ec — general use (30) (do not apply to brassicas after heads have formed or to beans after pods have formed); gamma-BHC dp — general use (30); mercaptothion wp, ec, dp — general use (7); mercaptothion/copper oxychloride/sulphur dp — general use (14); mercaptothion/mancozeb sulphur dp — general use (14); mercaptothion/pyrethrins dp — general use (7), cucurbits and tomato (1).

Bacterial blight: A bean disease with small, water-soaked areas on the leaves and pods, eventually forming large, brown lesions with yellow margins. Prevalent in wet or humid weather.
Control: Copper oxychloride wp (3).

PESTS AND DISEASES

Bacterial spot: A disease of brassicas and tomato. Purple-grey spots on brassicas and raised black spots on tomato foliage, enlarging.
Control: Copper oxychloride wp (3).

Bagrada bug: A shield bug with an orange cross on its back and orange and yellow spots and bands across the abdomen. It attacks a range of vegetables, but prefers brassicas.
Control: gamma-BHC ec, dp — general use (30) (do not apply after heads or edible parts have formed); mercaptothion ec — general use (10), bean and brassicas (7), tomato (1); mercaptothion/mancozeb/sulphur dp — general use (14).

Chafer beetle: A yellow-brown, medium-sized beetle which feeds mainly on young leaves and flower petals at night. Young and flowering vegetables are prone to attack.
Control: carbaryl wp — general use (14); gamma-BHC ec — general use (30) (do not apply after heads or edible parts have formed); gamma-BHC dp — general use (30); mercaptothion dp — general use (7); mercaptothion/mancozeb/sulphur dp — general use (14).

CMR beetle: Small to large beetles with bright yellow and black bands across the back. Their prime target is flower petals of beans, but may also damage other flowering vegetables.
Control: carbaryl/gamma-BHC dp — general use (30) (not on cucurbits or on brassicas after heads have formed or tomatoes after fruit has set); mercaptothion ec, dp — general use (7); mercaptothion/copper oxychloride/sulphur dp — general use (14); mercaptothion/mancozeb/sulphur dp — bean (14).

Crickets: Small to medium-sized insects which hop from plant to plant. Mainly attack young seedlings and transplants.
Control: gamma-BHC ec, dp — general use (30); mercaptothion ec — general use (10), bean and brassicas (7), tomato (1).

Cutworm: Usually grey, waxy worm-like grubs although there may be colour variations. They work in the upper soil surface and chew seedling stems at or just below soil level. Mainly active at night.
Control: chlorpyrifos ec — seedlings only; phoxim b; sodium fluosilicate b; trichlorfon wsp — applied as bait.

Damping-off: A disease which attacks overcrowded or inadequately ventilated seedlings or young plants and seedlings with poor drainage. Seedlings develop a soft, watery brown rot at or near soil level before collapsing.
Control: benomyl wp; Bordeaux wsp; captab wp; copper oxychloride wp — seedlings.

Diamond-back moth (larvae): A light-green caterpillar, which usually feeds on the undersides of leaves making holes. Main targets are brassicas.
Control: bromophos ec – brassicas (4); carbaryl-gamma-BHC dp – brassicas (30) (do not apply after heads or edible parts have formed); chlorpyrifos ec — brassicas (7); gamma-BHC dp — brassicas (30) (do not apply after heads or edible parts have formed); mercaptothion wp, ec, dp — brassicas (7); mercaptothion/mancozeb/sulphur dp — brassicas (14); trichlorfon wsp — brassicas (7).

Downy mildew: Pale green spots on upper leaf surfaces of brassicas, enlarging to become white-yellow with typical mildew growth on the lower surface. On onions there is a white to purple fungus followed by yellowing of the leaves. A similar fungus appears on the lower leaf surface of peas with yellow-brown spots on the upper surface. Small, yellow angular spots may appear on the upper leaf surface of cucurbits while the under leaf surface develops a grey form of mildew. Occurs in wet or humid weather or heavy dew.
Control: copper oxychloride wp, dp — brassicas, cucurbits (3), seedlings (–); mancozeb wp, dp — cucurbits, pea (3), brassicas, onion (14); mercaptothion/copper oxychloride dp — cucurbits (14).

Early blight: Brown or black patches with target-like circles on older leaves with yellowing of the surrounding leaf tissue. Mainly attacks potatoes and tomatoes.
Control: Bordeaux wp — tomato (3); copper oxychloride wp, dp — tomato (3); mancozeb wp, dp — tomato (3); mancozeb/sulphur wp — tomato (3), potato (14); mercaptothion/copper oxychloride/sulphur dp — tomato (14); mercaptothion/mancozeb/sulphur dp — tomato (14).

Fruit (pumpkin) fly: Attacks cucurbits. Small, brown flies with yellow bands or spots. Stings young fruits and lays eggs under the skin. Maggots usually kill small, immature fruits.
Control: fenthion ec — (10); mercaptothion wp, ec — (10); trichlorfon wsp — (10).

PESTS AND DISEASES

Greater cabbage moth (larvae): Young caterpillars are green, while older ones may have a white line and black spots on the back. Often found in groups where a web is spun. Main target is brassicas.
Control: bromophos ec — brassicas (4); carbaryl/gamma-BHC dp — brassicas (30); gamma-BHC dp — brassicas (do not apply after the heads or edible parts have formed); mercaptothion wp, ec, dp — brassicas (7); mercaptothion/mancozeb/sulphur dp — brassicas (14); trichlorfon wsp — brassicas (7).

Late blight: A serious disease of potatoes and tomatoes. Water-soaked or pale green spots on foliage which become almost black. Spreads rapidly under cool night and warm to hot/dry day conditions. Tomato fruits may have grey-green water soaked areas which develop into dark brown, wrinkled ones.
Control: Bordeaux wp — tomato (3), potato (14); captab wp — tomato (7); copper oxychloride wp — tomato (3), potato (14); mancozeb wp, dp — tomato (3), potato (14); mancozeb/sulphur wp — tomato (3), potato (14); mercaptothion/copper oxychloride/sulphur dp — tomato (3), potato (14); mercaptothion/mancozeb/sulphur dp — tomato (3), potato (14).

Leaf spot: Normally a minor problem affecting beet and Swiss chard.
Control: Remove badly infected leaves. There is no registered control but copper oxychloride wp, dp — (3) should be effective.

Millipedes: Smooth, hard segmented pests with many sets of legs. Feed on plant roots and tubers, mainly root vegetables and potatoes.
Control: If near soil surface, methiocarb b — used as a bait — may be partially effective.

Plusia looper: A pest mainly attacking bean pods and developing tomatoes. Green caterpillars feed on outside of pods and chew into tomatoes. They have a looping action when moving.
Control: chlorpyrifos ec — tomato (4); trichlorfon wsp, dp — bean (5), tomato (3).

Powdery mildew: A white powdery mould on the lower leaf surface which spreads to the upper leaf and covers the entire leaf. Most frequent in hot, dry conditions. It can attack a number of vegetables, but those most seriously affected are cucurbits and peas.
Control: benomyl wp — cucurbits, tomato (3); dinocap wp — cucurbits, pea (14); mercaptothion/copper oxychloride/sulphur dp — cucurbits,

pea (14); sulphur wp, dp — general use (–); triforine ec – cucurbits (1), pea (4).

Powdery mildew can be a serious disease unless controlled at an early stage. Crops most likely to be affected are cucurbits and peas.

Red spider mite: Microscopic red-brown, spider-like insects. Weaves a web on the underside of foliage causing bronzing and yellowing.
Control: diazinon ec — bean, brassicas, tomato (14); dicofol wp — bean, brassicas, cucurbits, pea, tomato (7); mercaptothion/mancozeb/sulphur dp — general use (14), bean, cabbage, cauliflower (10), Brussels sprouts (14), cucurbits, potato, tomato (21); sulphur wp, dp — general use (–) (should not be used on cucumbers or muskmelons).

Rust: A disease mainly affecting broad, bush and pole beans. Small white, raised spots which turn red after a few days then dark brown on the lower leaf surface. Extended periods of high humidity increase the risk of the disease spreading.
Control: mancozeb wp, dp — (3); mercaptothion/copper oxychloride/sulphur dp — (14); triforine ec — (3).

Rust mite: A microscopic mite which operates on the under-leaf surface causing bronzing of leaves and purpling of stems of tomatoes. Symptoms may appear similar to late blight.
Control: dicofol wp — (7); sulphur wp, dp — (–).

Septoria leaf spot: A tomato disease with water-soaked spots on tomato foliage, which enlarge to form lesions with grey centres and dark margins. Cool nights and hot days increase the risk of the disease spreading.
Control: Bordeaux wp — (3); captab wp — (7); copper oxychloride wp, dp — (3); mancozeb wp, dp — (3).

Short-horn grasshopper: Varies in size and colour. Mainly attacks seedlings and young plants of a wide range of vegetables.
Control: carbaryl/gamma-BHC dp — general use (30) (do not apply after heads or edible parts have formed); gamma-BHC ec, dp — general use (30) (do not apply after heads or edible parts have formed); mercaptothion wp, ec, dp — general use (10) (avoid spraying cucurbits if wet); mercaptothion/mancozeb/sulphur dp — general use (14).

Slugs and snails:
Control: carbaryl/metaldehyde b; metaldehyde b: methiocarb b; use as bait.

Stalk borer: Moths lay eggs in leaf sheaths and stems of sweet-corn and the larvae bore into the growing point and sometimes the lower stem.
Control: trichlorfon used in granular form.

Thrips: Minute insects which hide between folded foliage of many plants. Cause silvery blotches as they rasp foliage. Mainly attack beans, cucurbits, onions, peppers and tomatoes.
Control: bromophos ec — onion tops (7); carbaryl/gamma-BHC dp — general use (30) (do not apply after heads or edible parts have formed); chlorpyrifos ec — tomato (4); formothion ec — onion tops (14); gamma-BHC ec — beans (not after pods have formed); gamma-BHC dp — general use (30) (do not apply after heads or edible parts have formed); mercaptothion wp, ec, dp — bean (7), cucurbits (wp) (7), onion tops (7), tomato (1); mercaptothion/copper oxychloride/sulphur dp — general use (14); mercaptothion/mancozeb/sulphur dp — general use (14); sulphur wp — general use (–).

Wide-ranging and specific crop pests and diseases:
Wide-ranging:
Astylus beetle, chafer beetle, crickets, cutworm, grasshoppers, millipedes, slugs and snails and damping-off (seedlings).
Specific crops:
Bean, Broad: Aphids, rust.
Bean, Bush: Aphids, bacterial blight, CMR beetle, plusia looper, red spider mite, rust and thrips.
Bean, Lima: CMR beetle.
Bean, Pole: As bush bean.
Brassicas: Aphids, bacterial spot, bagrada bug, diamond-back moth and greater cabbage moth larvae, downy mildew, red spider mite and leaf spot of Brussels sprouts.
Carrot: Alternaria.
Cucurbits: Anthracnose, aphids, downy mildew, powdery mildew, fruit (pumpkin) fly, red spider mite, thrips.
Onion: Downy mildew, thrips. No registered home garden control for purple (alternaria) blotch or white bulb rot.
Pea: American bollworm, downy and powdery mildew.
Potato: Early and late blight.
Sweet-corn: Chafer beetle, stalk borer.
Tomato: American bollworm, bacterial spot, early and late blight, plusia looper, red spider mite, rust mite, septoria leaf spot, thrips.

Acknowledgement to: *A Guide To The Use Of Pesticides And Fungicides In South Africa,* compiled by J. Bot, Seugnet Sweet and Nora Hollings of the Plant Protection Research Institute.

Trade names of pesticides mentioned:
benomyl wp   Benlate.
Bordeaux wsp   Bordeaux.
bromophos ec   Nexion.
captab wp   captab.
carbaryl dp   Karbadust, Sevin.
carbaryl wp   Karbaspray, Sevin.
carbaryl/gamma-BHC dp   Blue Death.
carbaryl/metaldehyde b   Avisnail, Sluggem, Slug and Snail Bait, Protekta Snail Bait, Slaklok, Snailban, Sevin Snail Bait, Snailfix, Disa Snail Pellets.
chlorpyrifos ec   Dursban, Antsprey, Wurmsprey.
copper oxychloride wp   Koppersprey, Virikop.

PESTS AND DISEASES

D-phenothrin/tetramethrin aes   Garden Insecticide Aerosol.
diazinon ec   Dazzel, Kayazinon, Extermadazz.
dicofol wp   Kelthane.
dimethoate ec   Rogor, Aphicide, Protekta A, Aphikil, Pestox.
dinocap wp   Karathane.
fenthion ec   Lebaycid.
formothion ec   Anthio, Medit.
gamma-BHC ec   Dyant.
gamma-BHC dp   Lindaan, Lindane, Everdeath.
mancozeb wp, dp   Dithane M45.
mancozeb/sulphur wp   Milrust.
mercaptothion wp, dp, ec   Malathion, Extermathion, Malasol, Gardicide, Avigard.
mercaptothion/copper oxychloride/sulphur dp Rose and Garden Dust, Rosegard.
mercaptothion/mancozeb/sulphur dp   General Protekta Dusting Powder.
mercaptothion/pyrethrins dp   Python Dusting Powder.
metaldehyde b   Disa Liquid Snail and Slug Killer, Slugslak, Florusol.
methiocarb b   Mesurol Snail Pellets.
oxydemeton-methyl ec   Metasystox-R.
phoxim b   Volaton Cutworm Bait.
pirimicarb aes   Pirimor.
sodium fluosilicate b   Snylok, Cutworm Bait, Snykor Super.
sulphur wp   Thiovit.
sulphur dp   Vine and Dusting Sulphur.
thiometon ec   Ekatin.
trichlorfon wsp   Danex.
trichlorfon dp   Dipterex.
triforine ec   Funginex, Fungisprey.

Since this chapter was originally prepared it is possible that some pesticides have been withdrawn while others may have been added.
The use of these names does not imply endorsement or approval and no criticism is intended or implied for products which may have been omitted.

Glossary

Acid soil — Soils with a pH below 7,0, preferred by most vegetables.
Aeration — Free movement of air through the root zone of plants.
Alkaline soil — Soils with a pH above 7,0.
Axils (leaf) — The angle where the leaf is attached to the stem.

Biodegradable — Materials readily decomposed in the soil by micro-organisms such as bacteria.
Blanching — the exclusion of light to reduce green colour in plants or parts of plants such as celery, leek, witloof chicory and cauliflower.
Bolting — Premature production of flowers and seeds before crops are harvestable.
Broadcast — Sowing or scattering seeds or fertilizers uniformly over the soil surface instead of in rows.
Brassica — Members of the cabbage family, broccoli, Brussels sprouts, cabbage, cauliflower and kale.
Bottom-heat — An electrically heated pad to aid germination of seeds, rooting of cuttings and faster growth of seedlings.
Bowl — Raising the soil in a low circular mound with a depression for sowing, planting and watering. Also called a hill.

Catfacing — A disfiguration of fruit, mainly tomatoes, usually caused by sucking insects.
Chelate — A molecular form by which some nutrients, such as iron, are absorbed by plants.
Chlorophyll — Green colouring in leaves within plant cells.
Chlorosis — Lack of green colouring in leaves, often associated with nutritional deficiencies.
Clove — A segment of small bulbs produced by garlic and shallots.

GLOSSARY

Compost — Decayed vegetable matter used as organic matter to increase the humus content of soil.
Cool-season crops — Vegetables that do not normally thrive in summer heat such as Brussels sprouts, cauliflower, pea and spinach.
Cotyledon(s) — Seed leaf or leaves containing food for initial seedling growth.
Crop rotation — Growing plants in different locations in a systematic sequence to help control build-up of pests and diseases and to improve soil texture and fertility.
Crown — Growing point above the root where shoots develop.
Cruciferae — An extension of brassicas including radish, turnip, kohlrabi and swede.
Cucurbit — The squash family including cucumber, melon, pumpkin and watermelon.
Cultivar —— A 'variety' of a plant specifically cultivated by man, hence CULTIvated VARiety.
Cultivate — Loosening topsoil, usually to control weeds.
Cure — Drying skins for storing, such as onions.
Cv. — Abbreviation for cultivar.

Damping-off — A fungus disease causing seedlings to die either before or after emergence.
Determinate — Stem growth ceases when the terminal bud becomes a flower bud, usually associated with some tomato cultivars. Plants which are not self-stopping are indeterminate.
Dicotyledon — The seed has two seed leaves, such as beans.

Earthing-up — Heaping soil around plants to blanch (celery, leek), support (sweet-corn) or protect from exposure to sun (potato).

Fertilizer burn — Damage caused to plants by placing dry fertilizer on foliage or roots.
Field capacity — The amount of water soil can hold after draining off excess gravitational water.
Foliar feed — An organic or inorganic nutrient supply used in liquid form and sprayed or watered on foliage.
Friable — An easily cultivated soil.
Fungicide — A pesticide chemical used to control fungal plant disease.
Furrow — A shallow V-shaped trench made for seed sowing or irrigating.
F_1 hybrid — Plants of a first generation hybrid of two dissimilar parents. The main advantages being hybrid vigour, better uniformity, higher

yields, more disease resistance and possibly more resistance to pests. Seeds of F_1 hybrids should not be saved as the advantages are mainly lost after the first growing season.

Germination — The process of bringing seeds into active growth.
Growing medium — A specially prepared soil, soil mix or a soilless mix based on bark, peat, vermiculite or other soil substitutes, usually used for germinating seeds or growing young plants.

Hardening-off — Gradually exposing seedlings which have been started under some protection to open-garden conditions.
Hardy — Usually refers to plants capable of withstanding frost.
Hard-pan — An almost impenetrable soil layer below the topsoil caused by continuous shallow cultivation.
Herbicide — A chemical mainly used to control weeds.
Hilling-up — Mounding soil around the base of plants to give support and drain water away from the stem.
Humus — Decomposed organic matter which improves soil texture and fertility.
Hydroponics — Growing plants in nutrient solutions or in association with an inert material.

Immune — Free from disease infection because of total resistance (see also Resistant and Tolerant).
Indeterminate — The plant stem grows indefinitely as it has no true terminal point.
Infestation — The surface attack of pests.
Inorganic — Mainly refers to chemically produced fertilizers.
Insecticide — Chemicals or agents used to control insect pests, either on contact or through the body system (systemic insecticide).
Intercrop — To get maximum production by planting fast-growing and early maturing vegetables between rows of slower growing ones.

K — Symbol for potash.

Leaching — Loss of soluble fertilizers by percolation of water down through the soil, mainly nitrogen.
Leader — The central or main stem of a plant from which laterals develop.
Leaf-mould (mold) — Decayed leaves used to improve soil structure.
Leggy — Weak-stemmed and spindly plants caused by too much heat, plant food, shade or overcrowding.

GLOSSARY

Lime — A compound containing calcium and used to reduce soil acidity.

Micro-climate — The climate in a localised area, for example, a part of the garden mainly protected from frost.

Minor elements — Elements essential to plant growth but only required in minute quantities. Also called trace elements.

Monocotyledon — Seed with only one seed leaf, such as leek, onion and sweet-corn.

Monoecious — Plants with separate male and female flowers, such as cucumber and squash.

Mosaic — A virus disease that damages and kills plants.

Mulch — Materials such as hay, straw, leaves, grass clippings, sawdust, bark and black plastic sheeting used as a protective covering over the soil.

Multi-stem — A plant with two or more stems.

N — Symbol for nitrogen.

Nematode — A minute, invisible to the naked eye, pest which attacks a wide range of plants causing stunting and generally unhealthy growth. Also called eelworm.

Neutral soil — A pH of 7,0. Soils with a pH range of 6,8-7,2 are also referred to as neutral.

Node — A part of a plant stem normally producing leaves and buds.

Nodule — Small, round protuberances often seen on roots of legumes such as peas and beans.

NPK — Symbols of the three major elements, nitrogen, phosphorus and potash.

Nitrogen fixation — Transformation of nitrogen from the air into nitrogen available to plants through nitrification of bacteria on the roots of legumes.

Nutrient solution — A liquid containing some or all essential plant growth nutrients.

P — Symbol for phosphorus.

Parthenogenic — Fruit produced without fertilization, such as 'all-female' cucumbers.

Photoperiodism — The response of plants to exposure of light and dark periods of different lengths. See under 'Onion'.

Pinching — Removing the terminal bud or growing stems to stimulate branching.

Pricking out — Transplanting young seedlings.

Puddle — A mixture of soil and water in which transplants are placed to reduce the risk of roots drying out during planting.

Resistance — A plant's ability to limit pest and disease damage and to withstand adverse climatic conditions.

Residual — A continued effect over a period of time, often associated with the lasting effects of pesticides.

Respiration — When a plant absorbs oxygen from the air and releases water and carbon dioxide.

Rest period — A time when a plant is inactive.

Ridging — Pulling soil into a ridge at the base of plants, for example, potato ridges.

Rogue — An undesirable, inferior, off-type or diseased plant.

Root zone — The area of soil containing the bulk of a plant's roots.

Scald — An injury caused by sun, wind or frost.

Scorch — Brown, damaged areas on leaves caused by heat, lack of moisture or both.

Seedbed — Garden soil after it has been prepared for sowing seeds or putting out small transplants.

Side-dressing — Fertilizer applied close to the plant on the soil surface and watered in to make it available to roots.

Soil conditioner — Materials to improve soil texture or fertility.

Soil texture — The degree of sand, silt, clay and organic matter in a soil.

Spot-seeding — Sowing areas where previously sown seeds have either not germinated or have been lost following germination.

Spreader — Materials added to pesticides or foliar sprays for better distribution and coverage.

Staking — Tying plants to a stake to provide support, as with tomatoes.

Stagger — Planting alternately at equal or near-equal distances on either side of a middle line or row. May also apply to sowings and plantings at spaced timings.

Stand — A group of plants growing together in a given area.

Starter solution — A liquid fertilizer applied to plants at transplanting.

Sticker — A material added to pesticides or foliar sprays to give better adherence to the plant's surface areas.

Stopping — Usually refers to the removal of growing points.

Strain — A group of similar plants of the same species, usually with improved characteristics.

Susceptible — The inability of plants to withstand certain pest and disease attacks or adverse climatic conditions.

Systemic — A pesticide absorbed by a plant making it toxic to pests that feed on the plant. It also refers to disease which spreads through a plant.

Tilth — The condition of a cultivated soil.
Tipburn — Browning of tissue at the tips or on the edges of leaves and flowers.
Tolerant — The ability of plants to endure a specific pest, disease or adverse climatic condition while maintaining growth and production.
Topdressing — Application of soil, manure, compost and fertilizer to the soil surface when plants are growing.
Transpiration — Loss of water vapour from the aerial parts of plants.
True leaf — An ordinary leaf, unlike a seed leaf.

Variety — Closely related plants which are a sub-division of a species with similar characteristics, referred to as cultivars.
Vegetative growth — Growth of plant stems and foliage but not flower or fruit development.
Virus — A minute organism capable of causing plant diseases.

Water stress — Plants unable to absorb enough water to replace water lost through transpiration, resulting in wilting, temporary growth halt or even death of part of or the entire plant.
Wetting agent — A material used to increase the effectiveness of a liquid to wet a surface. There are also soil wetting agents.
Wilting — Drooping of leaves and stems as a result of lack of water, root damage, disease, heat or drying winds. Wilt is a disease and not related to wilting.
Wilting point — The point in decreasing soil moisture when a plant is unable to take up sufficient water for its needs, so causing a wilting condition.

Index

Bold figures indicate a major reference.

Acidity 19
Alkalinity 19
Alternaria blotch 112, 141
American bollworm 141
Anthracnose 142
Aphids 142
Artichoke, globe 60, 66, 73, **131**
Artichoke, Jerusalem **132**
Asparagus 66, 73, **132**
Aspect 10
Astylus beetle 142

Bacterial blight 142
Bacterial spot 143
Bagrada bug 143
Basic fertilizer programme **75**, 131
Bean, broad 66, 73, **83**
Bean, bush 60, 66, 73, **84**
Bean, lima 60, 66, 73, **85**
Bean, pole 60, 66, 73, **87**
Beet 60, 66, 73, **89**
Borecole (Kale) 62, 69, **135**
Bowls (hills) 27
Broad-bands 44
Broccoli 61, 67, 73, **90**

Brussels sprouts 61, 67, **92**

Cabbage 61, 67, 73, **93**
Cabbage, Chinese 61, 67, 73, **133**
Carrot 61, 68, 73, **95**
Cauliflower 61, 68, 73, **97**
Celeriac 61, 68, 73, **133**
Celery 61, 68, 73, **133**
Chafer beetle 143
Chicory, witloof 68, **134**
Chinese cabbage 61, 67, **133**
Climate **11**
Climatic regions **11-14**
CMR beetle 143
Container vegetables **60**
Containers 56-8
Continuity cropping 7, 52
Crickets 143
Cucumber 61, 68, 73, **99**
Cultivars 51, 64, **77-81**
Cutworm 143

Damping-off 144
Deep-beds **42-4**
Diagonal planting 45, 82
Diamond-back moth 144

INDEX

Direction of rows 10
Direct-seeded vegetables 35
Diseases 52, **141-8**
Double rows 45
Downy mildew 144
Drainage 55

Early blight 144
Eggplant 61, 68, 73, **101**
Endive **134**

Fennel, Florence **134**
Fertilizers 17, 75
'Field heat' 65
Florence fennel **134**
Fluid sowing **40**
Foliar feeding **22-3**
Frost 10
Fruit (pumpkin) fly 144

Garlic 69, **135**
Germination, temperatures for 33-5
Greater cabbage moth 145
Greenhouses **46-7**
Grey (waste) water 29
Growing by the moon **47-9**
Grow-bags 57
Growing medium 58

Hail 10
Hard-pan 16
Harvesting 65-73
Herbs 62
Hills (bowls) 27
Horseradish **135**
Humus 15
Hydro-growing **46**

Intercropping **53-4**

John Innes (JI) base 59

John Innes (JI) mix 59

Kale 62, 69, 73, **135**
Kohlrabi 62, 69, 73, **135**

Late blight 145
Leaf spot 145
Leek 62, 69, 73, **103**
Lettuce 62, 69, 73, **104**

Melon 63, 69, 73, **107**
Millipedes 145
Multiplier onion 137
Minor elements 18
Moon gardening **47-9**
Moon phases and signs 48-9
Mustard spinach **136**

New Zealand spinach 63, 69, 73, **109**
Nitrogen 18
Nutrient deficiencies 18

Okra 70, 73, **136**
Onion 70, **110**
Onion, multiplier 63
Onion, salad 63, 70, 73
Onion types **137**
Organic matter 15, 17

Parsley 63, 70, 73, **113**
Parsnip 63, 70, 74, **114**
Pea 63, 70, 74, **116**
Pepper 63, 70, 74, **117**
Pesticides **141**
Pests 52, **141**
pH **19**
pH references **19**
Phosphorus 18
Planning, advance 5-8
Plusia looper 145
Poor seedlings 39

157

Potash 18
Potato 63, 70, **119**
Powdery mildew 145
Precooling 65
Pumpkin 70, 74, **122**
Pumpkin fly 144

Radish 63, 71, 74, **121**
Rainfall 11
Records 8, 52
Red spider mite 146
Regions **11**
Respiration rates 65
Rhubarb 64, 71, 74, **137**
Root systems 20
Rooting depths 28
Rotation **20-2**
Rust 146
Rust mite 147

Safe (withholding) period 141
Salad onion 63, 70, 73
Salsify **138**
Seed storage 32
Seedbeds **35**
Seedlings 25
Seeds 31
Seedtrays 36
Septoria leaf spot 147
Shallot 71
Short-horn grasshopper 147
Short-lived seeds 32
Side-dressing **75**
Sites, choice of 9-11
Sloping ground 11
Slugs and snails 147
SNS (supplementary side-dressing) **131**
Soil crusting (capping) 32
Soil moisture 33
Soil pH 19

Soil temperatures for germination **34**
Soil wetting agents 28
Soilless mix 59
Sowing, fluid **40-1**
Sowing depths 76
Spacing **44-6,** 77
Spinach **138**
Square planting 45
Squash 64, 71, 74, **122**
Stalk borer 147
Starter solution 38
Storage times 73
Swede 74, **138**
Sweet-corn 64, 72, 74, **124**
Sweet potato **138**
Swiss chard 64, 72, 74, **125**

Temperatures 11, 52
Temperatures, storage 73
Thrips 147
Tomato 64, 72, **126**
Trace elements 18
Trade names (pesticides) 148
Transpiration 25, 37
Transplantable vegetables 35
Transplanting **37**
Transplanting shock 37
Transplants 25
Tunnels **46-7**
Turnips 64, 72, 74, **129**

Vegetables for containers **60**

Waste (grey) water 29-30
Water 10, **24**
Water requirements 24, **26**
Watercress 64, **139**
Water-efficient vegetables **28**
Watering methods **25-6,** 36, 60

Watermelon 73, 74, **130**
Wetter water 28-9
Wind 10
Windbreaks 10
Withholding (safe) period 141

Yields **81-2**

Zone watering 25-6